BURY ME WITH SOLDIERS

ONE GRUNT'S HONEST STORY ABOUT VIETNAM

BY

C. W. STANDIFORD

© 2003 by C. W. Standiford. All rights reserved.

No part of this book may be reproduced, stored in a retrieval system, or transmitted by any means, electronic, mechanical, photocopying, recording, or otherwise, without written permission from the author.

ISBN: 1-4033-9523-3 (E-book)
ISBN: 1-4033-9524-1 (Paperback)
ISBN: 1-4107-0657-5 (Dustjacket)

This book is printed on acid free paper.

To my children and grandchildren:

Seek peace and honor in everything you do.

And let no one take your freedoms, even if it means war.

Contents

Preface	ix
1 Born To Grunt	2
2 The Test Begins	11
3 The Wrong Kind of Training	23
4 Out of Order	33
5 Fatal Terrain	42
6 Echo Company	56
7 Cat and Mouse	68
8 Other Faces of War	81
9 Often Terrified, Never Bored	93
10 So Many Ways to Die	114
11 Into the Valley of the Shadow	125
12 Short-Timer	134
13 A Long Farewell to Arms	142
Glossary	151
Appendix	153

ACKNOWLEDGMENTS

Thanks…

To my good friend Ernie Cooke III, who helped me come as close as possible to what really happened.

To my editor, Judith St. Pierre, who understood the importance of this story and worked many hours to assist me.

To my wife, Deborah, who patiently waited for me to finish this task so I could get *other things* done.

Preface

In *The Art of War*, Sun Tzu wrote, "There is nothing more difficult than military combat." Mortal combat is the severest test of the human body and spirit, and since wars began, the line infantryman has suffered this trial in every one of them. In ancient times, enemies fought eye to eye. Modern man has invented ways to distance himself from the foe, but at times the individual soldier still makes eye-to-eye contact with the enemy. Any normal man who watches his enemy squirm in death will change. Any man who witnesses the deaths of his comrades will never again be what he once was.

This is an honest story of what one man saw, did, and felt as a soldier in Vietnam from 1967 to 1969. The events I describe are true, although I have had to reconstruct, and for narrative flow sometimes change, the sequence and timing. This story is how I remember those events and the people involved—and what they have come to mean to me.

There are many faces of war, and Vietnam was no exception. I have talked to veterans who were the only survivors of their entire company. There were countless sieges that were more brutal and fierce than the assaults I witnessed. My war was more like a slow, flesh-eating virus. Day after day I saw men mutilated and killed.

Hollywood can often distort reality to the point that some people think films like *Platoon* or *Apocalypse Now* are complete and accurate portrayals of the war. What I saw was completely different. In the two units I served with in the Third Marine Division, I never saw anything that would shame the people of this country. I witnessed no dishonor. We never burned a village or mistreated a prisoner. Drugs were taboo, and men fought to survive and to help their friends survive. Time after time integrity and self-sacrifice saved the day. There were incidents that did threaten the virtue of our units, but they were not assaults on the honor of the Marine Corps or this nation.

I have fought in only one war. In it, I witnessed the bravery of young soldiers, their unwavering stamina, their will to live, and their willingness to die. I lived with these men in conditions worse than anything I could ever have imagined in a protracted war that saw our country flounder pitifully and ultimately fail. With that failure, we, along with our nation, changed forever. Innocent, teenage soldiers—rock'n'rollers, rednecks, reluctant recruits—we went to fight an honorable fight to stem the tide of communism. But as the war dragged on, our music died, and the honor of this nation suffered a near fatal blow. Gone forever was our youth and innocence. For those of us who went and survived, the Vietnam War will go with us to our graves. And it will go as a task not completed.

I was one who returned, and I have written this book to honor the forgotten soldiers who served in America's longest tragedy, who answered the call of duty to their country, and who gave their lives for it. Our children and those who want to know the truth need to know about the brave and honorable men who made a valiant effort to win a war they believed was just.

If you can find a better group of men, bury me with them when I die.

Otherwise, bury me with soldiers.

In Memory

When the wind whispered low, "You must".
Youth answered, "I can". Emerson

2nd Lt. Morrell Crary
Salem, Oregon

Johnie Machau
Redmond, Oregon

Corporal Timothy Meeker
Redmond, Oregon

Gary Thomas
Davison, Michigan

1st Lt. Carl Myllymaki, III
Westerly, Rhode Island

PART I
CRUCIBLE 0311

Crucible: a severe test
0311: the numerical code for Marine Corps infantry

1
BORN TO GRUNT

One morning in the spring of 1966, our bus pulled up in front of Redmond Union High at 8:27 A.M. It had picked up kids from the ranches outside of town, and as usual, it was the last one to arrive. To make it to homeroom on time, I'd have to hustle to get through the usual morning bedlam. But when I entered the old brick building, the halls were hushed. All I could hear was the sound of sobs coming from students clustered in groups by the lockers. It seemed that something terrible had happened, but I had no idea what it was. A buddy walked by, long-faced and solemn.

"What's up?" I asked.

"Tim's dead," he said.

Timothy Meeker had graduated from Redmond High in 1965. He was one of those guys all of us looked up to. Soft-spoken, polite, an outstanding athlete—an all-American kid. To get a sense of his athletic ability, imagine trying to tackle a rolling log on a football field. He seemed to have been built of hard steel, with a good measure of concrete. If you hit him head-on, you'd probably wish you'd had a wreck with a logging truck instead. But Tim was humble about his athletic abilities, and he always had a quick smile for everyone. He made a perfect Marine.

In those days, Redmond, Oregon, was a small cow town. In our high school, cowboy boots and tight Wrangler jeans were fixtures of fashion. If you didn't own a pair of Justin cowboy boots, you were as out of style as you would be today if you didn't own a pair of Nike tennis shoes. We were common folks who didn't question our government or think twice about standing up to fight for our country. Tim was no exception. In 1965 the war in Vietnam was just beginning to heat up, and like a good American, he volunteered for the Marines.

Tim had been in Vietnam about three months when he stepped on a land mine. The blast took off one of his legs and one of his arms. His other leg had to be amputated. I couldn't imagine Tim without legs. What had it been like for him to find that his once strong, fast legs were missing? It seemed a cruel joke that hot, jagged iron could so gruesomely alter his young, vital body. Crueler yet was the pain he must have endured. I imagined mean little men gleefully poking and prodding his wounds, carving the flesh and bone of his stubs with dull, hot knives.

The Redmond community immediately began raising funds to fly Tim's parents to Oak Knoll Naval Hospital in California. They made several trips to Tim's bedside before he died six weeks later.

In 1965, Vietnam was a country I hardly knew existed. I knew there was a war going on there, but along with most of my classmates, I had no idea what it was all about, and none of us could comprehend its hideousness—or the hideousness of any war, for that matter. Although many of our fathers had served in WWII, they seldom spoke about their experiences. All we knew for sure was that John Wayne had won that war and that the American soldier was the defender of the flag, Mom, and her hot apple pie.

Young men like Tim kept going off to that obscure country, while the rest of us lived our lives as usual. We lived for Friday nights, when we would meet up with our girlfriends and drag the gut until we got bored and hungry. Then we'd head for the drive-in, where we'd sit for hours, talking and listening to the Beatles and the exciting new sounds of rock'n'roll. "I Wanna Hold Your Hand" was close to becoming America's new national anthem. The British had invaded our homeland with only the mop-headed Fab Four as infantry troops, and they'd pulled off the invasion without firing a shot.

In 1966 the speed of our young lives seemed to be increasing at an exhilarating tempo. Many of us lived by the minute, for the minute. Our days were full of music and sudden bursts of energy—energy that could mean trouble, but in the American way, more likely spelled success. Our futures stretched ahead of us, seemingly full of nothing but promise and opportunity.

Along with most of the kids from my school, I went to a spring dance sponsored by the Veterans of Foreign Wars. The dance floor was alive with bodies gyrating to "Louie, Louie," and the sidelines were packed with kids just listening to the music. I went outside and was hanging out with some friends when we saw an old schoolmate walk by.

"Hey, Keith," someone in our group called out.

Keith was another one of those chunks of walking concrete. I don't know if some young men had a secret diet passed down from cavemen to bulk them up, or if it was just one of those natural things that most of us never received, but if Keith hit you on the football field, it was another wreck with a logging truck.

Keith Berkoufer had graduated from Redmond High the same year as Tim. They were best friends, and after high school they had joined the Marines on the buddy system, which meant that they would train together in boot camp. Now Keith was home from Vietnam, and we had heard through the grapevine that he was going back for another combat tour.

Keith walked over to our little group of blood virgins, all of us still stupid about war. I was trying to figure out my own future, and I couldn't help but wonder why he was going back to a place that had killed his best friend. So I opened the conversation with a simple question.

"Mind if I ask why you're going back to Vietnam?"

Keith looked at me with eyes that weren't his own. After a slight pause, he said, "To kill more gooks." Then he disappeared into the dark parking lot.

The group fell silent. I felt uneasy and a little embarrassed. I hadn't understood his dark look and pointed, cold reply. Keith wasn't the same, and I was taken aback by the change. He was no longer a carefree teenager bouncing with the music. Even his music had changed: the notes were solemn and grim, like a funeral dirge played in a minor key.

From then on I felt a very big, dark cloud hovering over me, following me wherever I went. It was the cloud of uncertainty about the war, and I knew I would have to deal with it soon.

I was in my senior year of high school, but I still had no clue what I wanted to be when I grew up. My second-grade teacher had told my folks that I could be anything I wanted to. Most of the time I just wanted to be outside with a rifle or a fishing pole in my hand, so it was a challenge for teachers to hold my attention in school. My worst classes were chemistry and algebra, maybe because the same teacher taught both subjects. Mrs. Young was my mortal enemy. To this day I don't know what I did to get on her bad side. Maybe that's the only side she had.

Mrs. Young sported those brainy kind of eyeglasses. You know—thick as Coke bottles. Sometimes when I looked at her, I could have sworn she had taken the lenses out of a couple of microscopes and transplanted them into her eyeglass frames. I was afraid to get too close to her, but I thought that maybe there was a knob on the frame she could fine tune so that when she looked at me, she could tell instantly that I was making very little effort to master algebra and chemistry. She seemed like a talking test tube. She was all business, with no time to smile, let alone laugh.

One day in chemistry class, Mrs. Young was showing us how to handle test tubes. With a very serious expression and in her normal stern voice, she said, "Never point a loaded test tube at anyone!"

I thought it was the funniest thing the old crank had ever said, and I laughed out loud.

Mrs. Young glared at me over the top of her microscope glasses. "Mr. Standiford," she said, "I have never liked a class clown. Since you don't seem to be able to take me or this subject seriously, perhaps your time would be better spent in the hall."

The test tube incident put me firmly on the outs with Mrs. Young, and our relationship went downhill from there. But something also got into me, because in my last semester of high school I decided that I was going to make the honor roll.

I pulled it off. I actually studied and did my homework. But it almost backfired on me. My mom was thrilled that I'd made the honor roll, but frustrated that I'd wasted so much time. For a while I was afraid she was going to take me by one of my big ears and make me go through high school again, just to prove that I could graduate a little higher than the bottom of the class.

I don't know why it was so hard for me to sit and study. I guess some people are just born to be brainy, while others like me are born with intelligence but aren't smart enough to be intelligent. All I know is that I enjoyed the outdoors more than the indoors. Maybe I was born to grunt—to live in the elements, not study them.

With the shackles of school finally removed, I was a free man. I had only two problems in my life. One was no job; the other was the draft. I needed a job because I wanted to marry my high school sweetheart, Sally. The draft was the problem of every eighteen-year-old American male. I could get a deferment if I went to college, but for me that was out of the question. I'd had enough school for two lifetimes. I thought I was ready for the real world.

That didn't mean I was ready to go off to war in Vietnam. Lots of Americans were questioning why we were even there, and some had begun to protest. I kind of liked the protest songs—they had a catchy beat. I heard Peter, Paul, and Mary sing "Where Have All the Soldiers Gone" so many times that I began wondering that myself. But other than that, I didn't give it much thought.

Then the protest movement heated up. The evening news showed longhaired men chanting "Hell, no, we won't go" and burning their draft cards. The antiwar protestors were waging their own war—one for the hearts and minds of the American people—and their message gnawed at my soul. I'll never forget one poster I saw hanging from a now forgotten building. It read, "War is not healthy for children and other living things."

When I was growing up, my folks belonged to the First Baptist Church in the neighboring town of Bend, and most Sundays I pretty much had to attend church with them. If the weather was nasty, it was better than doing chores on the ranch, and a lot of kids from my high school went there. That's where I met Sally. The pastor was as boring as Mrs. Young, and from time to time some of us would sneak out and go down to the local café for sodas or coffee. Mom and Dad tolerated my truancy as long as I minded my manners and made it back to the church in time to ride back home with them.

Despite my sporadic attendance, I got saved and learned more about how God expected soldiers of the cross to conduct themselves. That's why the antiwar poster got to me. I wrestled with the sixth Commandment. The simple fact was that war killed people. For a fleeting moment I thought about becoming a conscientious objector.

But at the same time that the media was covering the antiwar movement, the news was full of stories about the innocent victims of the Viet Cong. Graphic descriptions of their atrocities disturbed our evening meals—women and children being tortured and murdered, village leaders being led off and never seen again. These reports made Uncle Ho look like the leader of a band of murdering thugs. What American wouldn't want to take them out?

Bumper stickers began spreading the message, "America! Love it or leave it!" Some guys took that seriously and headed off to Canada. For the first time in our history, the whole idea of duty to country was being widely questioned, and American society was coming apart. It was a bewildering time for those of us who faced the draft.

My dad was a man of few words, but we did have a few in-depth conversations about the war. I knew that Dad had lied about his age so he could join the army and fight in WWII. And my grandfather had lived with a damaged lung for years after being gassed in the trenches in WWI. With my family history of service to the nation, I knew I would not—could not—escape doing my duty. Dad thought draft dodgers were cowards who wouldn't stand up and fight for their country.

One of my cousins had booked it for Canada. One day he was a student at the University of Oregon; the next day he was in Canada. His dad had been a combat paratrooper in WWII, and his son's actions wilted his spirit. He couldn't figure out how this attitude had developed in the country. Hadn't Americans always been willing to pay the price of freedom? Now his own flesh and blood had run off rather than fight. My dad figured that pinkos at the U of O had brainwashed him.

Like Bob Dylan said, the times they were a-changin'—and for me they were getting more confusing all the time. I guess what puzzled me most was the lack of national zeal for the fight in Vietnam. If our country had been attacked, like at Pearl Harbor in 1941, the mood of the nation would probably have been very different. The issues in Vietnam weren't cut-and-dried like they were in WWII. In fact, I believe that most Americans didn't have any idea what our national leaders thought was at stake. At least I know I didn't.

But then I read an article in *Reader's Digest* about the "domino theory." The writer said that America was on a mission to contain communism and that Vietnam was the testing ground of our determination. That article convinced me that the war was a just one and that we should be involved. If we didn't fight communism in Vietnam, one day we'd have to fight it somewhere else—maybe even on our own soil.

Once I settled that in my mind, I had to decide what I was going to do. And I had to decide soon, or it would be decided for me. I didn't have a college deferment, and my father wasn't a senator. Just like the song said, I was no "fortunate son." My choices were to enlist or be drafted.

I was reluctant to hang around and wait for the draft to nab me. I'd heard stories about draftees who weren't motivated to fight, and I didn't want to end up next to a disgruntled soldier who could leave me face up in the dirt. I figured if you went into a fight, you went in to win, and I didn't want to find myself in a dangerous situation with someone who was half-hearted in that belief. That meant I didn't want to be in the Army.

I started checking out the other branches of the military. My friend Vern had talked to me about joining the Navy on the buddy system. I gave it some thought, but the Navy wanted your hide for four years, and I didn't want to commit for that long. Besides, the idea of getting stuck on some floating city didn't excite me. I'd been on the ocean only one time in my life, when my dad and I went salmon fishing. I got so seasick that just the thought of another voyage on the rolling ocean made me reach for the Dramamine. So it didn't break my heart that the Coast Guard was full. The Air Force was full, too. That left the United States Marine Corps.

By the spring of 1967 the war was in the news night and day, and many of my friends were going into the service. I was tired of trying to decide about my future, so one day I drove my old Chevy pickup to the office of the Marine recruiter.

The guy asked me a bunch of questions. I told him that I shunned the evil of booze and that I didn't smoke, although I had picked up the habit of chewing snuff. He was more interested in knowing that I wasn't a homo and that I had a clean record with the police. The worst thing I'd ever done—if you don't count being charged with truancy for skipping school to go fishing—was to get into a couple of fights at school. I also told him that I'd buckled down during my last term and made the honor roll.

That was it. It was a quick, clean deal. Faster than a flaming bullet from hell, I was in the United States Marine Corps. John Wayne was getting a new disciple, and I was even getting excited about the coming adventure. I guess I really was born to grunt. And three years in the Marines sure seemed a lot better than four years in one of the other branches. I felt the dark cloud lift. It was like someone had lifted a huge rock off my chest. I imagined Mrs. Young shaking her test tube at me and saying in her high-pitched, stern voice, "It's about time you got out of here. And I hope the Marines wipe that silly grin off your face."

I'd made the decision to fight, and now there was no turning back. Mrs. Young might not miss me, but as the future unfolded, I would come to miss even her.

I would have 120 days of delayed enlistment, which meant that I was in the Marines but that it would be four months before I had to report to boot camp. I'd heard stories about Marine boot camp. As we wound up our business, I asked the recruiter if the stories were true.

He nodded. "The best way to get through boot camp," he said, "is to keep your mouth shut and do what you're told."

Anyone who's ever been a teenager knows how hard it is to keep your mouth shut and do what you're told.

I went back to the ranch and dropped the news on Mom and Dad. Dad nodded his approval, and Mom almost hit the kitchen floor. A few days later I bought a ring and asked Sally out to dinner.

Sally and I went to our favorite restaurant, and I popped the big question.

"When I get home, we can get married and begin raising a family," I said.

"Oh, Wayne, I'm so happy," Sally said with a broad, sexy smile. "When you get back, we can have a bunch of kids, and life will be sweet."

I nearly toppled out of my chair. A biological urge overtook my brain, and I thought Sally might consider starting the family thing immediately. What I really wanted to do was to shed my virginity, and I thought maybe she might decide we could get married right now. It was a whole new branch of chemistry, and all of the sudden I was interested in learning it.

"Why wait?" I asked in a husky voice.

"Dream on, buster." Sally's tone changed faster than that speeding bullet from hell that had gotten me into the Marines. I bit my lip and took a gulp from my glass of ice water to put out the fire. I knew I would go to Vietnam with my virginity intact. It would be a burden, but one I would try to live with. I was going to save myself for Sally.

Now I had four months to enjoy myself without the cloud of uncertainty hanging over my head and following me wherever I went. Four months to roam and frolic like a lamb in summer pasture. The herdsmen would let me play for a stretch, and then I'd leave the peaceful meadow for boot camp.

Sally and I spent as much time together as possible. Because this is an honest story, I must tell you that I kept trying to find ways to shed my virginity. But Sally was strong, and she was determined to go to nursing school. Getting married right now was out of the question. She simply said, "When you come home, we'll …."

At that point I knew nothing about making love or making war. I was a raw recruit on both fronts. With my 120 days rapidly disappearing, it wouldn't be long before I received training for the war front. But I still longed for training on the love front. I'm sure you've heard the old saw "Where there's smoke, there's fire." Well, it's the absolute truth. I was smoldering and about to flash into a pillar of yellow flame. It's not easy to be engaged and fight fire at the same time. Sally and I were both from God-fearing families, but I sometimes wondered why in the world God gave the young this fire and then expected us to stay in this state of smoldering until the act of getting married. I was only beginning to understand just how weak my flesh was.

Vern was at the ranch often that summer, and when I wasn't with Sally, I spent a lot of time with him. My sister Debbie also had a friend around most of the time, and the four of us staged a mock war all summer.

One morning, Vern and I came up with a plan to dump pails of cold water on the girls. It was a simple strategy. My bedroom was tactically the perfect place to stage an ambush. Everybody, even the cats and dogs, entered our old ranch house through the back door, and the back porch was directly beneath my bedroom window. Vern would call the girls outside with some innocent request, and when they walked out the back door, I would hit them with the buckets of water. It went off without a hitch. The girls ended up soaked and screaming. We knew they would stage a counterattack—the only question was when. But nothing happened, and after a while we figured that maybe they'd forgiven and forgotten the cold-water bath.

Meanwhile, Vern and I planned a motorcycle trip. If we'd been a little smarter, we would have kept our plans a secret. On the morning of our departure, we jumped out of bed early. We ran by the girls' room, shook the door so hard that they screamed in terror, and then ran for our bikes—only to find that the tires were flat. The girls had finally struck back. As we walked in circles around our disabled get-a-way rigs, two smiling faces appeared at the back door. I chased them back in the house with a garden hose. It took us an hour to repair the old air compressor so we could pump up the tires. The girls harassed us the entire time with giggles and smart remarks, and when Vern and I finally got underway, we started laying plans for the next skirmish in the ongoing battle.

By the end of the summer, nobody had really won the war, but it had entertained the cows and chickens. I thought that the pandemonium might cause poor Mom to have a stroke, but as long as nobody got hurt, she put up with it. One thing about moms—they're born to worry. I suppose if it were up to them, there would be very few wars. Moms pay the price for man's inability to solve problems. One thing I knew for certain was that if my mother could worry me home, she would. It didn't help that Central Oregon had already lost some men in Vietnam and that Benny Dexter from Bend had been missing in action for more than a year. I also knew that Mom would pray every day for my safety.

It was a long summer of young love and youthful pranks. I was a happy man. I would get a real war behind me, come home a hero of democracy, and get married. Life would once again be summer pasture. Then I could put that fire out and really begin to live.

If I'd been able to see into the future, I would have bottled and sealed my youth. Then on my return, I could have taken it from the shelf and poured it into my vacated soul.

2
THE TEST BEGINS

It was amazing how quickly those 120 days disappeared.

When they were over, I went to Portland and boarded a jet for San Diego. This was my first plane ride, and for a kid straight off the ranch, it was more exciting than watching the cows drop their babies.

When we landed, snappy looking gentlemen greeted us with warm smiles and manly hugs.

That's the only lie I'll tell in this story.

The truth is that several large Marines with no necks met us at the airport. There were no smiles and absolutely no hugs. Even in the company of cosmopolitan travelers, their conversation was straight out of the comic strip *Alley Oop*. I tried to translate prehistoric Marine into English, but everything seemed garbled. I did figure out that we were supposed to stand at attention against a wall while we waited for the bus to pull around.

Young people looked at us sideways as we stood at attention. A striking blonde strolled by with her luggage. I guessed she was heading off to some vacation paradise. Along with a couple other recruits, I let my eyes wander.

"What are you maggots looking at?" Filtered through the drill instructor's clenched teeth, it sounded like an inquiry. I think he wanted to scream very loudly, but with all the civilians around, he decided to show some restraint.

Our eyes snapped straight ahead, and the blonde quickly became a faded memory. Life as I'd known it was about to change forever. This was not high school, and Mom was not around to pack my lunch.

The DI seemed to have something more to say, but there were too many people inside the terminal who didn't belong to our tour group, so he quietly herded us outside, where he could speak freely. And he did.

Even though we stood straight and silent, our escorts found reasons to scream and spit in our faces. Right then I decided that my decision to work for the federal government had been a big mistake. Unfortunately, mistake or not, here I was. The odds of sneaking out undetected were minuscule. Even if I got away, where would I go? And how would I get there? I didn't have a dime in my pocket. Then it hit me: That's why they told us not to bring any money with us. I couldn't hire a taxi for a getaway rig. I couldn't even make a phone call.

The bus pulled up, and the DI herded us at double time through the airport lobby. I've herded a few cows in my time, but this was insane. The Marines' screams intensified as we ran for the door of the olive drab bus. The outer limits had sucked us in, and there was no way back.

The DI's language would have angered my Mom to the bone. If she'd been on the bus, she would have grabbed that Marine by the ear and taken him to the bathroom for a good mouth washing. I could just see it: Mom leading a no-neck Marine by the ear. She might have had some trouble, though. I have good-sized ears, but that guy's ears were rather small, and it would probably have taken a pair of her kitchen tongs to snag them. I'm sure she would have figured something out, though. Over five years of struggling for my independence, I'd had some serious arguments with Mom, and she always figured something out. Now I wondered where she was when I really could have used her help.

The screaming didn't stop on the trip to the base. The Marines paced up and down the aisle of the bus as if they were looking for a fight. My eyes were locked in a stare to the front and were starting to dry out from not blinking. I think my heart even quit pumping. I was a sitting zombie—I didn't move, breathe, or think. I didn't want the wrath of those demented men falling on me.

We finally pulled into the base. With more foul language and high-pitched screams, the Marines herded us off the bus into the barbershop, where the barbers stood behind their chairs waiting for us. I'd heard about the famous recruit haircut, so, thinking I'd save the government some time, I'd had my hair done before I left the ranch. My hair was already short, so I saw no need for the barbers to remove what little I had left. My feelings didn't count, however, and as a reward for thinking ahead, I received a screaming set of teeth in my face.

"Think you're smart, maggot?"

I moved my head from side to side, a denial of any intelligence.

The screaming teeth proceeded to teach me how to converse with our new masters. "When you communicate with me, maggot," the DI shrieked, "you say 'Yes, sir!' or 'No, sir!' Do you understand me, maggot?"

"Yes, sir! Maggot, sir!" I yelled in the most unmaggot-like voice I could muster.

"What did you call me?" The DI's nose was almost on mine.

"You are Sir, sir"! I am Maggot, sir!"

The DI worked his way down the line of recruits waiting for their turns in the chair. One thing was for certain: We all had the same name: Maggot. Not Mr. Maggot; not Private Maggot. Just plain Maggot.

A bad moon had risen and the light was dim.

They kept us up all night, harassing us and screaming at us from point A to point B. They threw uniforms, boots, and underwear at us as if one size fit all. Amazingly, the Marine throwing the underwear was pretty good at distance sizing. I wondered what he'd done to deserve the fate of throwing underwear at half-naked bodies after midnight.

I don't know how they managed to find so much for us to do that we couldn't lie down and get some sleep. I've never been a night person, and after midnight I'm pretty much worthless. I suppose the screaming and name-calling did pump some adrenaline into my bloodstream, but by 0230 (which to me was still 2:30 A.M.) I was feeling very sleepy. I was walking toward some assigned position in a stupor when I stepped on the DI's spit-shined shoes.

What happened next is almost too obscene to describe. Even though this is a true story, I won't repeat the names he called me. I mean how much imagination does it take to figure out which four-letter words he screamed at the top of his lungs? Let's just say that after the DI finished with me, I was totally awake and able to get around the rest of the night with my eyes wide open.

Breakfast time finally arrived. Having acquired a healthy appetite on the ranch, by sunup, my stomach felt as if my throat had been cut.

We marched to the mess hall to the beat of the DI's screams: "Your left, your left, O ley, your left, right, left."

I don't understand how a man can yell all night and still have a voice in the morning. I thought the guy had to be getting tired of hearing himself scream. I would later learn that this was an art form and that only certain folks were born with the gift. It takes special breeding to replicate the DNA needed to produce a drill instructor. The most important genes are the ones responsible for strong vocal cords and the ability to look at everything from the most negative aspect possible. As far as I could tell, none of us had done one thing right since our arrival.

"Your left, your left, O ley, your left, right, left."

One guy had trouble with the cadence. Apparently, skipping "your right" threw him off. The DI halted our column to spend special time with the poor out-of-step miscreant. In most instructional situations in American schools, a student can be corrected with gentle words of encouragement and positive reinforcement. At USMC University, however, that wasn't the method of choice for individual instruction. The words the DI used to describe the wayward maggot's heritage and intelligence level could have only come from a manual written by the king of darkness.

It was amazing how those guys looked at things. I'd never been exposed to such nit-picky people. In their eyes, we couldn't even walk right. In less than twenty-four hours I'd learned that my parents weren't as dumb as I'd previously thought. I made a mental note to apologize for thinking I knew more than they did.

After the DI finished his one-on-one tutorial, he ordered us to march. Everyone got in time, and we managed to make it to the mess hall without further problems.

When we smelled the cooking bacon and the other fine fare of the Marine mess, our stomachs growled in anticipation. Everybody knows that male teenagers take great delight in making fun of noisy body functions. But now we couldn't even do that, because we'd been told to stand with our eyes straight ahead and our mouths shut. The Marines were rapidly taking the fun out of being a gross male teenager.

We entered the mess hall and were handed a metal tray with neat little compartments. The bacon and eggs were mere inches away. But just as I held out my tray for service, the DI bellowed "Hard right!" and marched us to a row of tables. At each setting was one neatly placed orange.

This is fine, I thought. *A little appetizer before the main course.*

Then the DI barked the best command of all: "Eat!"

As you would expect, we all began to peel our orange. But with that simple, logical act, the DI went lunatic on us. He jumped up on a table and screamed and spit as if he'd been possessed by a demon. I managed to figure out that it upset him to see anything wasted in the United States Marine Corps.

Finally the demon gave control of the DI's body back to him. Calming down, he politely explained how we were to eat our oranges. We were to eat it peeling and all and not leave one drop of juice on the table.

I could see now that the DI had a split personality. He was a raving madman one minute and soft-spoken, sane person the next. It was odd how rapidly he could transform himself. The real scary part was that this man would control us for eight solid weeks. I suddenly realized that although we were the taxpayers and he worked for us, there was absolutely no way to fire him.

I looked at the orange. *Well, okay,* I thought. *I can do this. Whatever it takes to get to the bacon and eggs.*

The bitter taste of the orange rind stung my lips and tongue. I swallowed hard and finished the appetizer. I was willing to do anything to get a meal.

Now in his sane mode, the DI walked quietly up and down behind us. When every recruit had finished his orange, he ordered us to stand at attention. I figured we would execute an about-face and get back in the chow line. I would soon learn to never figure. The DI again bawled "Hard, right!" and marched us out of the mess hall. Breakfast was over.

Now I really wanted to go home. Stories about how to get out of the military flashed through my very numb skull.

After our fine meal we were marched to the company street and ordered to stand at attention. One by one our names were called, and after a resounding "Here, sir!" we were issued our dog tags. When we all had our tags, we were told to memorize our service number. We were given one hour.

"You will know this number like you know your name," the DI said. He walked up and down the line as he pounded in the importance of learning our number. "When you go to bed at night thirty years from now," he assured us, "you'll be able to recite your number as if it were your middle name."

He was right. More than thirty years later, I can rattle off my service number as quickly as I can my name. I can give you this number in the heat or in the cold, in bed or standing up. It might well be the very last thing I say in this life: 2274609...2274609.... 2274609. If I say it more than three times on my deathbed, just go ahead and shoot me.

We finished memorizing our number and then went out for physical training. This is where the Marine Corp shines. PT was a major part of our daily existence at War U, and the physical science of it quickly became very clear to me. The weight of the human body makes a very inexpensive workout tool. Sit-ups, push-ups, and pull-ups all use the natural force of gravity to make your muscles strain.

"The more we sweat in peace, the less we bleed in war," they kept yelling at us. If we were lying supine, they wanted to see our stomach muscles quiver as they pulled us to a sitting position one more time. If we were in a prone position, they wanted to see our arms shake as we tried to do just one more push-up. If we were hanging from a bar, they wanted to see our faces contort as we attempted to pull our skinny butt, fat butt, or muscle butt up and place our skinny chin, fat chin, or muscle chin over the bar one more time. They would push us just enough to see if we could sweat blood.

It's impossible to remember when we finally got to go to bed that first day at boot camp, but I think we hit the rack soon after the sun set. I was in the middle of a very nice dream with the blonde I'd seen at the airport, and she was just taking me in her arms when the lights and screaming jolted me awake.

This was a whole lot different from the crowing rooster back at the ranch. There wasn't even time to stretch and yawn. I hit the floor with both feet and got dressed on the run. There seemed to be screaming teeth everywhere, and if you hesitated one microsecond, they were in your face.

The rest of the days of our lives in boot camp were much like the first twenty-four hours. Whether we were marching, exercising, doing laundry, or eating chow, screaming teeth followed us everywhere we went and instructed us in everything we did.

It took me a few days to realize that the Marines' game was to see if they could break our minds into itsy-bitsy pieces. The body could take their abuse, but the mind is a fragile thing. One simple word could shatter your self-esteem, and these guys had a whole lexicon of crushing words: maggot, faggot, scum, puke...and ones I never did get to look up in the Marine to English dictionary. I think each recruit had to make a conscious decision not to let a DI break him. I know I did.

I decided that I would not let them hammer me so far into the ground that I couldn't get back up. Just like the recruiter had told me, the key to survival was to keep your mouth shut and do what you were told. If I did that, I knew I'd come out of boot camp in one piece and, with luck, still of sound mind.

I played a little game that helped preserve my sanity. I remembered watching movies about the French Foreign Legion when I was a kid. Hollywood showed Legion recruits enduring terrible training just so they could become part of that fierce fighting force. I wrapped my mind around that fantasy and envisioned myself gladly wading through hell just to become a member of an elite group. The DIs could run me until I dropped and make me do push-ups until my arms felt like sticks. They could even splatter their angry spit in my face. I wouldn't quit. I would survive.

But some recruits wouldn't.

If a recruit couldn't handle the mental strain, he was sent to a special "motivational" platoon, where they tightened the screws further. After the recruit completed that special training, he had to start boot camp all over again. Conceivably, a recruit who couldn't adapt could spend his entire enlistment in boot camp. That didn't make much sense to me. Obviously, the goal was to get out of there as soon as possible.

A few of the recruits broke. One guy cut his wrists in an attempt to end his stay in boot camp. One started wetting the bed, and another one cried at night.

A few fought back. The day before we were scheduled for hand-to-hand combat training, one especially ballsy guy talked back to the DI and refused to follow orders. The next day they used him for a punching bag to demonstrate the various blows. The recruit began to bleed from his mouth and nose, but he never asked for mercy. After the bloody exhibition, he was removed from the platform, and we never saw him again. The incident was one more proof positive that if you bucked the system, you paid a heavy price. What I didn't understand was that if the Marines were looking for tough guys, why had they just dragged one off the platform?

A few recruits ran. One jumped over the fence, never to be seen again. Another one, this time a sailor, got fed up with training and decided to leave government employ by jumping the fence. Sadly, he had neglected to think through his escape plan. When he landed on the other side of the fence, he found himself on the Marine Corps side of the base, where the military police quickly apprehended him. Rather than return him to the Navy, they decided he could train with the Marines. The one time I saw him running with a platoon of Marines, he looked quite dismayed.

Our DI pointed him out. "See that scumbag? Maggots like that don't belong in the service." He went on to say that we had a higher calling than miserable civilians and that, as the chosen few, we'd have to defend pukes like that.

They washed our brains with that kind of stuff every chance they got. And as absurd as it was, I began to believe the things they stuffed into my head. They were going to transform us, and there was no fighting it. At the slightest hint that you weren't conforming, you were pounced on, and then verbally and physically reeducated. If that didn't work, off you went to the dreaded motivational platoon.

My worst day in boot camp was when the DI nearly broke my thumb. There was a proper procedure for everything. When we were ordered to line up in formation for roll call, or for any other reason, we had to extend our left arm and point our fingers straight out, with the thumb lying along the index finger. Apparently I didn't put my thumb where it belonged, because suddenly the DI grabbed it and bent it back to my wrist bone. The crack of bone and tendon nearly brought me to my knees.

"Keep that thumb down," the DI yelled in my face.

"Yes, sir!" I screamed back.

The pain was excruciating, and I was so angry that when he finally released his grip, I thought I was going to lose it. But as visions of the motivational platoon danced in my head, I managed to conceal my anger and endure the pain.

My thumb had been severely sprung, and it ached the rest of the time I was in boot camp. Even years later I couldn't open a car door with my left thumb because every time I tried, it would snap and grind. Whenever my thumb would act up, I would cuss that particular DI.

Ironically, my best day in boot camp was when they taught us how to fight with a bayonet. On the farm I'd stuck several cows to relieve their bloated stomachs, and that was enough for me to know that I never wanted to see an enemy's ugly stomach stuff all over me. It was dawning on me that even though I might have been born to grunt, I was not a born killer. I knew I didn't have one violent bone in my body. I'd been raised to never start a fight, but once one started, I could defend myself. I wasn't a softie, but I didn't have a hard heart, either. I was just an average American kid my country had called to war. That's what nearly all of us were, and I guess that's why they had to work so hard to turn us into trained killers. In boot camp cries of "Kill!" accompanied everything we did. The transformation was something I'd never thought about or expected.

Despite the constant brainwashing, I still wasn't interested in drawing human blood. But even with this attitude, I listened closely and practiced the strokes with the intention of doing the best I could. We learned about vertical strokes, horizontal slicing, forward thrusts, parries, and all the other ways to kill a man up close. The instructor claimed that thrusting cold steel into a human body was the perfect way to kill. He proudly cited the bravery of warriors of old who had stood toe to toe with the enemy and slugged it out with spears, knives, and swords. He said that if a Marine ran out of ammo, his best line of defense—or offense—was the bayonet affixed to his rifle. It was a given that Marines never retreated. We were told that running away was a cowardly act and that Marines were not cowards. Death should always come before dishonor.

Once we had perfected the strokes, we were paired off for more practice. The pugilist sticks were padded on both ends, but they could still smart. Wearing football helmets to protect what was left of our brains, we went at each other with slices and pokes. If our opponent didn't counter our thrust properly, we were awarded a kill or a wound. Somehow, I was never wounded and made several kills. I was becoming quite good at faking and then thrusting with a kill stroke to the stomach or placing a solid butt stroke to the head.

When we were allowed to rest, the instructor told us some war stories about Marines who had fought with rifle butts and bayonets. I grimaced at the thought. I would not have done well as an ancient warrior. If I was going to die in this—or any—war, I preferred to go quickly. I didn't want to endure the internal bleeding that would drain the life out of me. The thought of turning pale and gasping for air in front of my adversary sent a chill through my body. I shook off the thought. We were supposed to think positively. We were to be the dealers of death, not the recipients.

After the break we were lined up and paired of for the grand finale. We were going to have a contest to see who was the champion of bayonet fighting. Looking around at some of the gorillas in the platoon, I guessed it would be an interesting fray. Sure enough, I was paired with a mean-looking Marine who owned more muscles than I could ever purchase.

I squared off with Mr. Muscles and waited for the whistle to blow. His attack was clumsy and slow. I stepped back, ducked, and countered with a stroke to his heart. I'm not bragging, because I was just as surprised as he was.

One by one I defeated my opponents and moved into the final round. My last opponent was a buddy, also from Oregon. He was a tall kid, well put together and with very long arms. We faced off. He came at me with calculated speed. Using a horizontal butt stroke, he rattled my head and sent me to the ground as a dead man. I got up, shook my head, and then his hand. He'd won first place in the competition, and I'd managed to come in second. Second place in competition with muscle-bound apes was okay by me. I was happy to see two Oregonians defeat tree-top-primates from distant paved jungles. The DI gave both of us a nod of approval, which was a reward in itself. I'd finally done something right.

When we weren't marching, running, training, or getting yelled at, we attended classes. The classroom was a peaceful haven. Unless you nodded off, the instructor was quite pleasant. All we had to do was sit and listen, and it really felt good to sit. It almost made me long for those high school days—almost. If I'd been less of a knothead in high school, I could be sitting in some college classroom instead of in a room full of green-clad jugheads just like me.

One class was on the Uniform Military Code of Justice and the Code of Conduct. The class was interesting. The main thing to remember was that in the event enemy forces captured us, we were to give only our name, rank, and service number. The instructor told us some gruesome stories about Marines who held fast to this code even when bamboo spikes were driven up their fingernails or they were being skinned alive. I wondered if I could live up to the code. To be honest, I hoped to God that I would never have to find out.

For some reason, one DI was concerned that a couple of recruits wouldn't pass the exam, so he took me aside and asked me to help them cheat on the test. For a moment I thought about the consequences if I declined his request. He could make life even more miserable for me, or he could simply beat the stuffing out of me. Or he could do both.

Bracing myself for the onslaught of words and fists, I said evenly, "Sir, the private respectfully declines your request." I didn't want to show any sign that I was afraid or that I was taking a weak stand on my conviction.

The DI stared at me with eyes I couldn't read. Maybe he was just testing me, or maybe my stand surprised him. Without a word, he made a right turn and walked away. My body relaxed, but I was worried that it wasn't over. We marched into class and took the test. To my relief, no retribution came.

After the class sessions, we hit the obstacle course. The leap over the mud pit was the most memorable event. We carried our rifles when we jumped, and the trick was to throw the rifle out in front of your body. That increased the momentum of your flying sack of bones and allowed you to fetch up dry on the far shore. I'll never forget the DI standing over one poor recruit who had come up short and landed facedown in the mud. It was bad enough to be eating mud without the DI standing over you cursing and wisecracking.

When my turn came, I ran as fast as I could for the pit. Thrusting my rifle in front of me as instructed, I flew through the air clutching my weapon, cleared the mud, and landed in the gravel. Since my hands were outstretched, they did most of the braking as I slid to a stop. I was dry, but the hide had peeled off almost every finger, and I was bleeding profusely.

We had been told repeatedly to report injuries immediately. I hated the thought of confessing what had happened. I assumed that the DI would belittle me in front of everyone before he sent me to the aid station.

"Sir, the private requests permission to speak, sir!" I barked in my boldest bark.

"What is it, private?"

I displayed my bloodied hands and expected the worst. To my utter shock, he simply told me to get the tail end of my donkey to sickbay.

When I walked into the infirmary, I was met with the most obscene screaming I'd heard so far (I think). Two corpsmen were demanding sexual favors from a small, frail-looking Marine, who was sitting on a chair, sobbing. It didn't take me long to figure out what was happening. The Marine had apparently decided that enough was enough and had tried to convince the medical team that he was a homosexual and therefore unfit for duty. The two corpsmen weren't buying the Marine's story and seemed to be having more fun with him than two cats playing with a wounded mouse.

I felt sorry for the Marine, but not sorry enough to butt in. It seemed to me that it was easier to live through boot camp than it was to try a ploy like that to get out. I knew I didn't want to go home and tell my Dad or my friends that I didn't want to be a Marine anymore. On the other hand, if someone were to wake me up and tell me that it was all a bad dream, I would have booked the fastest jet out of this weird nightmare.

Now all I wanted was to get my fingers fixed up and get the heck out of there. I was afraid those two perverted doctors might start in on me, and I was not in the mood to lie about how happy I was to be in the Marines.

Finally one of them looked my way and saw the blood dripping on the floor. Strolling over to me, he reached down and raised my hands up for inspection. He shook his head and pointed to a table. I walked over to the medical workbench, and in no time I was bandaged and on my way out the door. The harassment of the Marine picked up where it had left off.

On about the sixth week, we left boot camp for the rifle range at Camp Pendleton, where we were to spend one week learning everything there was to know about the Marine's best friend, the M-16 rifle. Every Marine had to know how to use this weapon. It didn't matter if you were a cook, a truck driver, a pilot, or a bookkeeper, the Marine Corps required every member of its organization to be at least a marksman with the grunt's rifle.

The week was a nice change from the regular routine, and for the most part it went well. I had just one little problem, but it was a simple one that was immediately corrected.

Every morning we had to stand at attention for roll call. (They wanted to make sure that no one had given them the slip during the night). It was always in alphabetical order, and my name was always one of the last to be called, but when the DI finally called my name, I didn't respond. Maybe it was my one little act of defiance. Maybe I was tired of having to be accountable for every moment. Maybe I was thinking about home, or about Sally. Whatever it was, it cost me.

The DI called my name again, and as loud as I could, I yelled, "Private Standiford. Here, sir!"

An ominous silence descended on the squad bay.

"Private Standiford, front and center!"

I ran to the prescribed distance from the DI and stood at attention. The very big black sergeant looked at me with cold, steely eyes. I never saw his fist coming. It hit my face with a solid blow. The floor hit my body with another solid blow. Dazed, but not out, I jumped up and stood at attention. I wobbled a bit, but I tried to act like nothing had happened.

The sergeant's white teeth loomed in my face. "Now do you know your name?" they bawled.

"Yes, sir! Private Standiford, sir!"

"Fall in!"

I ran back to my position. My face was numb. The DI had placed the blow just under my nose on the right side of my cheek. It was well placed: no blood, no black eye. The guy knew what he was doing: I was once again part of what was going on around me. For a fleeting moment I missed Mrs. Young. And I wished I had a loaded test tube to point at that DI.

The next evening there was an incident that became bloody. I don't know what caused the uproar, but it ended with a recruit being called into the DI's office. The screaming was the worst I'd heard coming out of the DI's mouth so far. He always seemed to be angry, but this was an anger I hadn't seen before.

We were never—never!—to look directly in the DI's office. Unfortunately for him, the human eye can see out of its corners, and that's how I saw what was going on. The recruit stood at attention as the DI verbally worked him over. Then a muscle-bound Marine was called in. It was Mr. Muscles. He began to work over the smaller man, and the recruit went down. It was an ugly picture. After about five minutes the bloodied recruit came out of the office. Mr. Muscles followed him, his nostrils flaring. He walked with a swagger, like a lion that had just devoured a deer.

I felt nothing but contempt for the man I'd beaten in the bayonet contest. As far as I was concerned, only a sadist would beat someone who was not allowed to fight back. I understood why we were thumped on occasion, but there were times when the DIs enjoyed their work a little too much. When he used a recruit for a contract beating, the DI crossed the line. I was plenty pissed about this situation. I couldn't understand why Mr. Muscles would agree to beat the stuffing out of a fellow Marine or what a recruit could have done to warrant this kind of action. To my mind the only thing this beating proved was that any man can beat the snot out of another if there's no chance he'll fight back.

Graduation day came at last. We were paraded out under the colors of the American and Marine Corps flags. I must admit that I felt a certain amount of pride as they played the Marine Corps hymn and the national anthem. They had molded us, but we had survived. We were about to hatch from squirming white maggot eggs into United States Marines. It was quite satisfying to be called a Marine. No matter what the future held, we had become brothers of an elite outfit that had made us sweat, bleed, and endure just to earn the name—Marine.

Right after the graduation ceremonies, we were assembled and read our orders. The DI went down the list of names. The orders of more than 90 percent of the names read "0311 Infantry, Wespac, Republic of Vietnam." I wasn't surprised at all when I heard my orders. I was headed off to Infantry Training Regiment and would be following the crowd to Vietnam. As I said before, it appeared that I was born to be a grunt.

I couldn't believe the human inflection in the DI's voice as he bade us farewell. He seemed almost in tears. "Some of you will not come home," he said. "Others of you will come home in pieces, and some of you will give arms and legs for your country. No matter what happens, always remember that you are Marines!"

He knew what we were going into, and I know that it tugged at his emotions that day. Maybe it even bothered him that he and the other drill instructors had done their part to turn us into cannon fodder. Whatever he felt, he didn't stick around to talk about his feelings. He gave us a smart salute, did a quick about-face, and disappeared. His job was done.

Ours was just beginning.

3
THE WRONG KIND OF TRAINING

Compared with boot camp, infantry training was a breeze. It was physically challenging, but it seemed easier without the added mental stress of some demented DI screaming in our faces. Now the instructors seemed to be reasonable human beings, and they addressed us as Marines.

Mr. Muscles and I ended up in the same platoon. I didn't even want to talk to him and avoided him like the plague. The memory of him swaggering out of the DI's office behind the bloodied recruit still bothered me. In boot camp they'd taught us that whoever owned the most bullets would inherit the earth, and Mr. Muscles obviously thought that went for his muscles too. But the way I saw it, there had to be some compassion along with the muscles before I could respect the person packing them. At times Mr. Muscles would throw me a mean, sideways glance, so I think he knew how I felt about him. Fortunately, I'd rung his bell pretty hard in bayonet training, and maybe he thought there was more to me than met the eye. Whatever he thought, I was happy to snub him when I had the chance. On the other hand, I'd never challenge him, because I knew if he ever got his hands on me, I'd be instant dog meat.

Infantry training was really kind of interesting. We learned more about combat and how to move and fight as fire teams and larger units. We did a couple of forced marches, then spent about a week in the field playing war and eating C rations and another one firing every weapon in the Marine inventory. My favorite was the hand grenade. It was a simple and reliable cyclone of a weapon—just pull the pin and throw the thing at whatever you wanted to blow to hell. I came to admire the sound it made—*whump!*—and how it rattled the earth. My next favorite was the M-79 grenade launcher, which could lob a grenade that looked like a pregnant rifle bullet. This weapon would send a grenade round farther than you could throw a grenade by hand. It made a less impressive whumping sound, but it was still an amazing weapon.

Some of the instructors told us hairy war stories. One of them had a bad stutter, and we heard he hadn't been born with it. One day when he was on patrol, an RPG removed all traces of the two men next to him. When the dust settled, he was the only thing left. There wasn't even a pool of blood on the ground where his buddies had been. From that day on he never spoke normally again. He was a comical sort, but his humor drove home some serious and important points.

Another story we heard was about an instructor who had lived through several tours in Vietnam only to be killed by a hand grenade while instructing a clumsy trainee. The irony of that man dying while teaching others to kill wasn't lost on me.

We heard plenty of stories about Vietnam, and by the time we finished infantry training, I think most of us thought we were ready to lock horns with the enemy. We'd learned a little about pain by then, and we knew that different people have different thresholds. One person can get a tooth pulled without painkiller; another will beg for mercy when the dentist walks in the room. In the mortal contest we were about to enter, each of us would discover our own threshold of pain.

One thing they couldn't prepare us for, however, was the threshold of fear. Marines were to be fearless, so we were told, but our stuttering instructor was proof that even though fear could be conquered, it couldn't be entirely removed. Our instructors couldn't teach us live with fear, and there was no weapon in the Marine arsenal that could destroy it. I would learn that on my own. I would also learn that the Marines had given us the wrong kind of training for the war we were about to see in Vietnam.

The war wasted no time in finding me. It began immediately when our C-130 landed in Dong Ha and incoming mortars chased it down the runway.

"Bail! Bail!" the crew chief hollered over the noise of the engines and the exploding rounds.

The tailgate was lowered, and we were told to get off the plane as it taxied. The plane was moving slowly, so that part wasn't risky. But black smoke from the mortar rounds was puffing right behind the plane, and that was enough to shake, rattle, and roll us into high gear. I followed the lead and double-timed it off the plane. I don't know if the gunners timed this attack just to welcome us to the war, but whatever was going on, it obviously wasn't a time to stand around asking questions.

I suppose the gunners were laughing at us as we hustled for cover with our sea bags bouncing on our shoulders. The exploding rounds came closer to the plane and closer to our high-stepping bodies as we ran hard for the trenches. Some men dropped their bags; some fell down and flattened themselves on the ground in an attempt to avoid getting hit. I felt like a little mouse caught between a hawk and a buzzard. I hit the trenches headlong. I went one way and my sea bag went the other.

Over the exploding rounds, I heard a loud groan and a louder string of obscenities. "You broke my leg! Damn it, you broke my leg!" (I've toned his language way down because I know his mother didn't know he talked that way.)

Word came down the trenches that a Marine had dived into the trenches and landed on a captain's leg. Some of us weren't sure why the captain was so angry. A busted leg was the same thing as a ticket home. Someone suggested that maybe the captain was already on his way home and that the broken leg would delay his trip back to the real world. At any rate, it was clear that the captain was in pain and one very mad Marine.

Ten minutes after the incoming stopped, a siren sounded. By the time we crawled out of the trenches, the C-130 had already escaped back into the safety of the air. My orders were to report to Third Battalion, Third Marines, so I threw my muddy sea bag over my shoulder and silently fell in with the group. For some reason I looked back over our escape route from the plane. A sea bag lay shredded from a direct hit by the incoming. It didn't take much imagination to see what mortars could do to a Marine.

I took a look around. One thing that stood out about this place was that everything had its own shade of green. The only things that weren't green were the ground, the sky, and the flying red, white, and blue.

We headed toward a sea of tents off in the distance, and when we reached them, I walked around looking for battalion headquarters. It was like swimming against a tide of dirty, scruffy Marines. Many looked as if they'd been in the elements for months. After some searching and asking for directions, I finally saw a sign that said Third Battalion Headquarters. Even the sign was green. I set down my bag, dug out my orders, and walked into the tent. A Remington raider sat behind his typewriter. He didn't even look up.

"Private Standiford reporting for duty as ordered!" I said.

"Have a seat," the clerk said. He pulled a sheet of paper from his typewriter and reached for another one.

Maybe to him I was just another body for the battalion, but I was here to serve the flag, Mom, and her apple pie. He was about as friendly as a fence post, and I was a bit put off by his attitude. The welcome on the airstrip had already tested my attitude, and now this aloof noncombatant was testing it a bit further. But like a good dog, I waited for my master's attention.

Finally the clerk thumbed through my papers. Looking at another folder, he told me I'd been assigned to Lima Company.

Acting a little distant, I nodded my head, as if I approved. Not that I had any say in the matter, but I figured I could play his game.

"You need to go to supply and get your war gear. When you leave here, hang a right and you'll see the supply tent. When you're finished, report back here, and I'll tell you where to find your squad tent."

The clerk in supply was the Remington raider's twin. Both had a knothole for a mouth. I've had more interesting conversations with a porcupine. I didn't understand the lifestyle here at Dong Ha. I'd soon find out what made them so testy and taciturn, but at the moment I was so fresh that my ignorance stood out as boldly as my new boots and utilities.

After I got everything I needed to wage war, the battalion clerk directed me to a tent where some lounging Marines were reading, playing cards, and smoking. When I walked in, I could feel their eyes on my white face and clean utilities. No one spoke. I've never been what you'd call a social butterfly, but this cold welcome set me back a few yards. I'm not sure what I expected. Maybe a simple handshake, a slap on the back, or words of encouragement like "Welcome to the war, sucker!" Anything but silence.

I busied myself with arranging my pack and cleaning my rifle. I also knew that I had to fill my canteens and sort my boxes of C rations. The only thing I didn't know was how much food I should carry. I'd been handed a bandoleer of ammo, so I figured that was the amount I needed to take. I looked around to see how grenades were carried and mimicked what I saw. Still left alone by the others, I went looking for a water supply to fill my canteens.

I'd just returned to the tent and sat down on my cot when someone casually mentioned incoming. The group came alive, and I followed my tentmates to the bunkers. The blasts seemed almost to entertain the hunkered men I was with. I guess they weren't concerned because the rounds weren't landing close. Having just outrun the mortars on the airstrip, I was glad to be in a bunker instead of out in the open, so I think I felt almost as casual as the others. At least I tried to act relaxed.

The incoming lasted about twenty minutes. After the all clear sounded, we meandered back to the tent. No one had yet spoken to me or acknowledged me in any way. I figured I would just stay quiet and try to figure out why everyone was so aloof. This was one of those times when silence might be a good teacher, so I decided to watch and listen.

About an hour after dark, a hard-looking sergeant summoned me and assigned me to stand watch on the perimeter of the base. He gave me the basic orders: Don't fall asleep and stay alert.

After a while, another Marine showed up. He would be my "hole buddy" for the night. We were handed extra ammo and grenades, and then I followed him to the wire marking the perimeter. I walked silently beside him, waiting to see if he would talk to me. After we'd gone a few yards, he asked me my name and where I was from. I gave him the information and asked him the same questions.

He said that his name was Steve and that he was from Louisiana. His casual southern drawl kind of relaxed me. It was like some kind of music to my ears—not elevator music, but a soothing twang of country mixed with down-home feeling. It was the first conversation I'd had with a fellow grunt since my arrival.

I was walking kind of funny because the humidity was causing me some discomfort in the area where I got spanked when I was born (not my face). Humidity can wreak havoc in places that seldom see the sun.

"It's the skivvies," Steve said.

I looked at him with a blank look. I didn't understand his comment but was afraid to ask a stupid question. My baboon butt was getting more uncomfortable with each step, but I still didn't make the connection.

I worked those four words over and over in my mind until it finally dawned on me that the skivvies had to go. Mom's advice to not leave home unless you're wearing clean underwear didn't apply in this country. The Celtics of old fought in their birthday suits; we would fight without underwear. It's still a mystery to me what the heck the Celts were thinking when they decided to fight in the raw. It was intimidating enough just to have Marines stare at my clean utilities. I couldn't imagine meeting my new tentmates with nothing on. How could a naked guy act tough and ready to fight? I was thankful that I didn't have to run around Vietnam bare-ass naked.

About midnight the rain came down, not in buckets but in barrels. I thought I'd need scuba gear just to breathe. Mr. Nelson, my high-school science teacher, had drummed it into me that water will always seek the lowest level. That night proved it without a doubt. Mr. Nelson would have been very proud. I could see him standing at the blackboard scratching out strange, shorthand science symbols with white chalk. I knew he was a member of the National Guard, so I wondered if he'd ever conducted experiments on flood control in foxholes.

At 0100 hours the water was up to my knees. Steve cursed, climbed out of the hole, and threw himself under a poncho. I took that to mean that I was to stay awake while he hid from the rain.

By 0200 the water was up to my neck. Fear of dying kept me in the hole. I was so cold that my shivers set off a small tidal wave, and I was shaking so hard that there was no way I could have fired my rifle. On the upside, I figured I'd be a hard target to hit.

The flares, tracers, and occasional small-arms fire kept my eyelids spread wide. The new, strange sounds of conflict were almost enough to make me forget the cold water. I wonder how my friend Vern was doing in the Navy. At that moment, it wasn't hard to figure out which one of us had the higher IQ.

The sun took its sweet time finding the eastern horizon. That night still holds the record for the most miserable night I've spent on earth so far. I'll never forget it. I don't know which was worse, the cold or the sounds of night war. I would never have guessed that a body could get so cold in that hot, humid place.

That night I had lots of time to think about what it really meant to be a grunt. If you'd like to simulate the experience, there are a couple of things you can do. First, simply enlist in the Marines. They will even pay you for it. Or you can get the gist of it in your own backyard. I'd recommend the second option because if you get tired of the simulation, you can simply go in the house. If you chose the first option, however, it's kind of hard to change your mind in the middle. Option two will require you to do the following:

1. Dig a chest-high hole in your back yard.
2. Hire 25 cold-blooded killers (if you can't find that many, 3 or 4 will do).
3. When it's raining hard, spend the night in the hole.
4. Put a bucket on your head.
5. Do not bring a flashlight or gloves. Wear only light clothing and a poncho.
6. Do not leave the hole for any reason. If you have to urinate, do so in the hole.
7. Do not sleep. Tune all your senses for any movement towards your position.
8. Do not talk, lest you give your location away.
9. Do not ghost-fire your weapon. It could be your friends coming inside the wire.
10. Guard your home.

The cold-blooded killers will attempt to sneak up on you, so you must stay awake. If you fall asleep, their contract states that they must slit your throat. If they are able to creep past your position, it also requires them to kill your family. The bucket over the head is to simulate wearing a helmet. Make sure the bucket has a good top seam that will collect water. When you happen to look down, the water will pour out of the seam and run profusely down your body. Also, you might want to try this on the hottest night of the summer. Try to wait until there has been a good hatch of mosquitoes.

Do all this, and you'll have a good idea of what my second night in Vietnam was like.

When the sun finally came up, there wasn't a cloud in the sky. Steve peeked out from beneath his poncho and laughed when he saw my head sticking out of the water. I tried to smile, but my teeth were hammering against one another so hard that I couldn't do anything but chatter and shiver.

"Let's get some chow," Steve said, still smiling. His soothing drawl couldn't relax my shuddering body.

When I tried to slither out of the hole, I had serious trouble getting my body to obey my brain. My hands were wrinkled and drawn. I couldn't hold onto my rifle. If that's how a newborn baby felt, I was glad I would only be born once. Everything hurt when I moved.

Step by step I began to limber up. The morning sun was already hot, and steam rose off me as we made our way to the chow tent. I must have looked like a mobile Swedish sauna. Steve laughed all the way to the tent.

Finally he quit laughing and asked me a serious question. "Why did you stay in the hole with all that water?"

"I didn't want to die on my second night in country," I said.

He laughed again, but I was dead serious. It may sound odd, but I couldn't think of a screwier way to get wasted than to get killed before I had one week under my belt. It would set a poor example of how to survive. I could just imagine everyone talking about how I got killed on my second day in Vietnam. I didn't want to be the topic of that conversation.

Steve and I hit the chow line at the same time as the others who'd been out on the perimeter. We were all wet and muddy. The steam rose, but the mud stayed. At least now, I didn't look so new. I noticed that several Marines had numbers written on the front of their helmets. Crossed-out bigger numbers were followed by smaller ones. One said 28, another 32. One was 4. I asked Steve what they meant.

"Short-timers," he said. "These guys are getting real close to getting out of here."

Although men from the other branches did twelve months, the Marines served us up for thirteen. With 365 days in a year, that meant I had to do at least 395 days. Three hundred ninety-five minus 2 left me with 393 days. I knew it would be a spell before I started marking the days on my helmet. I found it amusing to follow the numbers. It was kind of like gunfighters notching their guns after a kill, only in this case, the smaller the number, the better.

Steve and I had breakfast together that morning. It consisted of powdered eggs, reconstituted milk, and some kind of imitation meat. If an army really did travel on its stomach, I hoped we were taking a very short trip. Steve disappeared after breakfast, and I never saw him again.

I went back to the squad tent and took off my skivvies. I understood that this was a personal thing—to wear or not to wear underwear—but I was amazed that this had never been discussed during training. The government could have saved a million dollars if the Marines had taken the time to sit us down and explain that this was a war where you could leave certain things at home.

I was able to take a catnap. I'd never even slept in dirty pajamas before I joined the Marines, but in Vietnam, I would sleep a lot of nights in a mud-caked pair of pants and a sweat-soaked shirt. The only discomfort I had at this particular moment was soggy feet.

Someone shook me awake and told me to saddle up. We were moving out.

For some reason we were in a big hurry to get to wherever we were going. No one seemed to know where that was exactly, except the guys in the lead, and they weren't talking. We were packed into trucks for the fast, dusty trip. At some X on the map we left the trucks and began a rapid forced march to the north. This hump took place on my third day in Vietnam.

I couldn't believe how the sweat could flow from my lily-white body. With the heavy pack, rifle, helmet, and flack jacket, I felt like I was about to commit spontaneous combustion. I came around a small clump of vegetation and saw a corpsman bending over a gasping Marine, who looked as though he'd been in the oven way too long. I paused to watch, but someone from behind commanded me to keep moving. I guess the guy didn't know I was having trouble staying on my feet. My legs wobbled, and I came very close to joining the prostrate Marine. And we'd only been humping for about thirty minutes.

I was out of gas, running on vapor. To this day I don't know how I kept myself upright. I know I would have felt better if they would simply have shot me between the eyes and let me sleep forever. If they expected me to keep moving much longer, they might as well write my mom and tell her that I died and wouldn't be coming home. Or they could tell her that I managed to live but wasn't recognizable. I was about to turn into a very large, dried prune.

Finally the hell-bent march came to an end. I guess we'd humped about five hot, green miles. By the time we reached our destination, I'd seen at least three Marines overcome by the heat. I now knew that it had been wise to leave the skivvies behind. The added discomfort would probably have been the straw to break this ol' camel's back. Even so, I was surprised that I hadn't succumbed. Maybe I really had turned into a dried prune and had just rolled down the trail. Whatever outer or inner force kept me going, I was thankful. I was the new guy, and it would have been a humiliating start for my outfit to see me floundering and gasping for air.

Someone with a voice of authority ordered me to break right and take ownership of an old foxhole. I complied, grateful I could stop moving. After I peeled off my sweat-soaked flack jacket and guzzled some water, I began to feel I might live through this heat from hell after all. I thought I was in good physical shape from all the training, but no amount of training in the States could prepare a body for this kind of torture. I wondered if I was the only one in pure misery. I looked around to compare my condition to the others. A lot of them looked as if they had just completed nine holes of golf.

From the looks of things, this place had been occupied before. There were old foxholes, caved-in bunkers, and rusty concertina wire strewn between the dirt and the jungle. I overheard a couple of guys talking. The Army had been here and had been overrun. They also said that North Vietnam was visible on the distant horizon. Other than these two clues, I had no idea where I was. I knew we had moved north, but if everyone around me disappeared, I would be lost.

Trying to hide from the sun, I found a sliver of shade in the foxhole. My pulse and body temperature began to return to normal. Then a piece of moving shade glided over my little pit. I looked up to see a Marine lieutenant standing over me.

"Welcome to the Washout," he said with a slight grin. "I'm Morrell Crary."

I got up and shook his hand.

I was still having some trouble with the cold reception I'd received. Most of the men in my company simply didn't acknowledge my presence. I hadn't expected a brass band and red carpet when I arrived, but the cold shoulder made no sense. I figured since we were in this war together, it sure wouldn't hurt to talk to one another. I didn't understand the aloof attitude of the old salts towards new guys.

Now someone had finally been friendly.

Lieutenant Crary was older than I, with gentle, handsome features. He was soft-spoken but seemed to be a serious officer, and he obviously cared about his men. As we talked, he asked me where I was from. I told him I was from Redmond, Oregon. When he told me he was from Salem, I didn't feel quite so lonely anymore.

Having this man smile and talk to me revived my body and spirit. It was strange to talk about home.

We'd been allowed a ten-day leave before we had to report for infantry training. I called my folks from the airport in San Diego and told them I'd be in Portland in about two hours. It was a two-and-a-half-hour drive from the ranch to Portland, so I got there before they did. The speed of jet travel was still a mechanical marvel to me.

The ten days were a blur. I spent as much time with Sally as I could before it was time for a sad round of good-byes with her and her family. I promised them I'd take care of myself and not do anything stupid to get myself killed. I repeated the ritual with my family. My brothers, Brian and Brad, were still too young to know what was going on, but Debbie wiped away her tears and hugged me good-bye. My dad was still proud and my mother was numb, but still praying.

With our good-byes said, I had stepped back aboard the time machine and flown back to Camp Pendleton for infantry training.

I hadn't thought about home at all since I hit the runway at Dong Ha. The vortex of Vietnam had sucked me in so deep that it was like living on the border of night dreams and the thing we call reality. It had been a fuzzy couple of days, but now my conversation with Lieutenant Crary was bringing me out of that swirling existence.

I wished we could have talked longer, but the lieutenant soon shifted the conversation to the business at hand. He told me to clean my weapon and then start remodeling the foxhole. He said we were in a contested area and that I should be ready for anything. Our platoon would go out on patrol in the morning. I nodded. I'd recovered from the miserable march and was ready to push Ho Chi Minh back to his commie homeland.

4
OUT OF ORDER

"I'll get someone over here to be your partner," Lieutenant Crary said just before he left. "Listen to him and pay attention."

Ten minutes later a sour-faced Marine named William stood over me as I dug in the earth. He sat down and lit up a smoke. I found it kind of amusing that he didn't offer to help with the project. He was black and I was white, so maybe this was payback time for the slave days. I almost asked him, "Stop for water, boss?" but thought better of it. The guy had arms bigger than my thighs, and I guessed that one hit from him could send me into a very long coma.

I dug and dug. William watched and exhaled. I still didn't smoke, so there was no reason to stop digging. With my limited knowledge, I used my limited common sense. I thought the deeper the hole, the better the hole.

Finally William said, "You're the dumbest shovel operator I've ever seen."

I stopped digging, stood back, and looked at what I'd done. I'd just dug a hole so deep that we would need a ladder to get out of it—not a real practical way to make a fast exit. I began back-filling the hole.

William shook his head and lit up another smoke.

Nightfall came slowly at first. As it descended, kamikaze mosquitoes attacked in bloodthirsty formation. The government-issue bug juice seemed more of an attraction than a repellent. One particular piece of anatomy they seemed to like was my lips. Soon my upper lip was itching and burning. Then it swelled to the size of a walnut shell. I guessed my third night in this rancid country was going to be another night of tribulation.

Suddenly it was very dark. Something had devoured the sun and spit out an absence of light. I couldn't even see the wall of our foxhole. My ears strained for any hint of movement. All I knew for certain was that my hole partner was still breathing and my lips were on fire. I thought about the stories of men who had fallen asleep in the jungle. They were sent home with their throats cut. I listened for the sounds of the little yellow men. Were they at this very moment creeping toward my hole with their blades drawn?

It is unholy in the dark in the jungle in the night. In the dark there are eyes that can see, while your eyes cannot. In the jungle there are things that creep and things that crawl. These things hunt for you. In the night, you can hear your heart and feel the raw edge of your nerves. Tension expands and contracts. Adrenaline runs at 200 octane and flashes into 90-proof fear.

That night it was very dark in the jungle.

Another bad moon had risen and the light was black.

Something moved out front. I flipped the safety off, ready for the little yellow men. I was shaking and vibrating inside.

"What was that?" I whispered.

"Quiet!" William said.

The fluid in my spinal column gelled.

I'd just made my second blunder as a new guy. My question could have been answered by cold quiet steel or hot hellfire.

All night, things moved. We'd been taught that the worst thing you could do was to fire at those ghostly movements. The flash of your fire would mark your spot. I would learn that was their game—draw your fire and then sneak in and slash or shoot. It was a contest of nerves, a game of hide-and-seek in the dark, in the jungle, in the night.

Finally, after what seemed a month of darkness, the sun rose like a red rubber ball. It had been a long night of tracking things unseen. To confirm that I hadn't just heard things, I asked William if the sounds had been real. He nodded.

We ate cold C rations, and I attempted to make a hot cup of coffee. On my first hunting trip with Dad, I'd acquired a taste and need for the hot black liquid. I thought about that wet, cold day. Dad had handed me a lumpy cold cheese sandwich and a steaming cup of coffee. I was ten. Those hunting trips were the best part of being a boy. I loved the woods and the challenge of finding the quarry. Maybe this was just another hunting trip.

We got word to get ready for the morning's patrol. Some Marines bunched up as we gathered, and the gunny told them to spread out. "One round will get you all," he said. It was a phrase that would become as routine as the heat.

We spread out. With our flack jackets and helmets, I thought we looked like a line of tall turtles All of us held our rifles in a casual fashion, but the grenades and ammo hanging off us were proof positive that this wasn't just another deer-hunting trip. A tall black Marine was holding an M-60 machine gun over his shoulder, and his A-gunner was laden with a spare barrel and many rounds of ammo. This was further proof that we were hunting warm-blooded men.

Lieutenant Crary walked down the line and spot-checked us, passing quickly by the old-timers. One of them made a wisecrack, and the lieutenant grinned. As he approached me, he was still smiling from the quip and looked relaxed. He asked if I was squared away. I told him my weapon was clean and that I had 500 rounds of ammo. Peering around my left side, he inspected my grenades and nodded.

We moved out and crossed the concertina wire one at a time. No one spoke. Lieutenant Crary was about two men ahead of me in the column. I had no concerns. I didn't know what to be concerned about. I simply followed the guy ahead of me. I don't remember being even a little bit nervous.

We hadn't been beyond the wire for ten minutes when things fast-forwarded into a frenzy of gunfire, yelling, and explosions.

"The lieutenant's been hit!" someone screamed above the sounds of battle.

I saw Lieutenant Crary go down. When the burst of fire exploded from the tree line, I hit the ground and hugged it, trying to make myself instantly skinny. I froze facedown in the warm dirt. I wanted to get up, but there was something from the earth holding me down. The cold tentacles of an unseen apparition had me pinned.

Finally I was able to look up. A ring of defensive security had already formed, and I could see a corpsman working on the lieutenant. Lying under a tree, he looked peaceful, but the frantic movements of the corpsman told a different story. I buried my face in the dirt again. I tried to breathe, but the air stuck in my throat. I don't know how long I lay there.

Finally I got up and began cranking fire at an unseen target. The bark from the trees flew as my rounds cut away their skin of life. Changing the clip, I cranked more fire into the trees. Out of the corner of my eye I could see the tall black Marine advancing with his M-60 machine gun. The gun barked in cadence with his strides. His face was contorted with anger. It was like watching a ballet of fire dancing on fire. His helmet and body shook with each long burst.

"Grenade!" someone yelled.

The explosion shook the earth, but the gunner didn't stop.

In midstride he pointed the gun down to the ground, and the fury erupted from the gun with two long final bursts.

"There, you bastards!" he yelled.

"Grenade!" I heard someone scream again.

My stomach went sideways in my throat. I glanced over at the lieutenant again. The corpsman was working in what seemed a frame-by-frame flurry of peculiar motions. The lieutenant still lay peaceful, much too peaceful. A chopper hovered overhead while another spread gunfire into the tree line. I was told to hustle out and help form a security perimeter for the landing chopper. The entire North Vietnamese Army could have been charging, and I would never have seen them. It was as if I'd somehow become detached from what was going on around me. I couldn't keep my eyes off the men who were carrying the sleeping lieutenant toward the chopper. I couldn't believe what I was seeing. I had no idea what his wounds were, but somehow I knew they were mortal. Frame by frame the movie rolled.

The lieutenant was placed gently into the bowels of the bird. I didn't hear the blades hammer at the air as the chopper lifted off. I saw, but I didn't hear. "Red," our burly radioman went by me firing his .45 at our rear. More gunfire erupted up the line, but it seemed a distant, unimportant event. I stood frozen in my confusion.

Then a slow, relentless, yet blurry comprehension dawned on me, an understanding of the setting in front of me. I felt the vomit rise and stick in my throat. I tried to hold it back, but I gagged and it spewed out onto my feet. Someone grabbed me and forced me into the column of retreat. I knew I was about to break up, so I fought for sanity until I crossed the wire. Then I broke formation and ran for my foxhole.

I fell into the pit and bawled like a baby until the dry heaves attacked me with rage. I gagged for air. I was sick to my stomach and sick in my heart. I wanted the last twenty minutes to be sucked back into the ghoulish time machine. I wanted out of this war. I felt conquered. I was puny, unfit to be a Marine. Marines were devil dogs, not bawling pups.

Marines passing by ignored my sobs and gags as I made my way unarmed down desolate streets lined with laughing demons poking my sorrowful soul with spears. I couldn't even pray to God for help. I felt cut off from him, cut off from everything. I couldn't think or move. I was caught in a spiritual battle for my courage—for my very being—for my right to breathe the same air as the men around me. A brave lieutenant had died, and I, a miserable sack of flimsy bones, had survived. Death in war had come, and it was out of order. I was out of order.

I don't know how long the struggle went on in my little pit of despair. Mother earth held me patiently until I became calm and wooden. No one came to help me in my struggle. They knew I had to travel alone. Finally I climbed out of the pit and found my helmet. I must have thrown the thing when I fell into the hole. No one looked at me, and I looked at no one. They had already made their own lonely journey and knew there was never a welcome-back party.

I needed water for my soul, but death stood between me and the well.

The next day there was a brief memorial service. The words of the chaplain sounded like a distant echo. There were three other rifles standing on their bayonets, but I didn't ask about the other men killed in action. I hadn't seen their bodies and hadn't even known about their deaths. They must have been killed on that same patrol, but I couldn't remember anything but the death of the lieutenant. I felt like a very old teenager with a jagged memory.

The service seemed so futile, as if it had nothing to do with the man who had just died. Afterwards, someone said that the lieutenant had a wife and probably a baby by now. It was the last memorial I attended in Vietnam. Never again would I stand solemn in the church of combat. It was the evil one's first victory over my faith.

As it does sooner or later everywhere in the world, the sun finally set once again over the Washout. Tonight would be another very long, dark night for the scruffy Marines camped there. In this war we were the knights of grunge. We had no shining armor, just mud and sweat-caked battle dress. In a very short time, fatigue hacked at our bones, and the dirt penetrated our skin. The bugs were back, and the fight to stay awake became a test of the will.

We knew for certain that Charlie was out there, and we knew that he was watching us. The shadow noise was much the same as the night before—until screams descended from heaven with a thunderous noise that threatened to devour our minds. I'd heard nothing before, and have heard nothing since, so hideous and foreign to my ears.

I thought that heaven and earth must have turned upside-down. The sounds of hell aren't supposed to come from the heavens. What we heard could have come only from Satan's domain. The Bible talks about war in heaven. From the sounds that came from the sky that night, Satan must have just dropped one of the biggest weapons from his evil armory in his war against the Almighty.

After a long screech and the shrill sound of brimstone groaning, the fierce explosion shook the center of everything that had become our world. It almost threw my partner and me from our pit. Then in the awful silence that followed, the cries crawled out of the dark, slowly at first, then in an uncontrolled frenzy. High-pitched moans, screams of agony, wails of consuming pain rose and fell. Marines called for the corpsmen so many times that it sounded as if everyone else in our hundred-man company was torn and bleeding.

"What should we do?" I whispered to William.

"Stay put and be ready," he whispered back.

I wanted to ask what had fallen on us, but I was learning the importance of silence in the night. One misplaced sound could spell death. I could feel the faint tremble of my partner's body vibrating against the hole. I too shook. Questions were racing through my mind. What fierce weapon had hit us? Were we the only ones left alive? Would Charlie come charging out of the jungle to finish the job?

The sounds of shuttling feet pounded hard against my ears. The cries pounded harder. I wondered if I would join the chorus of agony in the dark. To be honest, I had to fight hard to keep fear from consuming me. I flipped the safety on and off so many times that my trigger finger was getting sore. My ears ached for relief from the sounds of those in pure, constant pain. It would be better to burn energy and fire at the enemy than to sit here in the dark listening to the groans and wails of those still alive. At least a fight would cover the sounds of torment piercing the dark.

But the sounds of running feet and moans of pain hung tight with the dark. It was like being in a horror movie with the giant screen blacked out. The soundtrack held your attention while the screams frothed your imagination. The night had a life of its own, immoral and immortal. There would be no peace until the blessed daylight came again.

When at last the light of day drove back the sounds of the night, choppers battering the air finally subdued the conspiracy of the dark. The soundtrack of the night was followed by a frame-by-frame moving picture of the dead being loaded into the womb of a mechanical angel. Bodies, in bags and under ponchos, lay ready for the shuttle. The wounded lay prostrate and bandaged, while the corpsmen moved about incessantly, trying to ease their pain.

My eyes locked onto the scene of dull green misery. Choppers landing, Marines collecting the dead, corpsmen caring for the wounded—all seemed to be in the same peculiar motion I'd seen when the lieutenant was killed. I rubbed my eyes in an attempt to overcome the sensation. I wanted to turn away, but some force kept me watching the scene.

After less than four days in this possessed land, I was rapidly being hardened like steel. I'd been put in the heat, and I was now ready for the cooling part of this unholy quenching. The process was a slow but methodical alienation of myself from myself. The estrangement allowed me to stare at the body bags lined up on this dirty, naked piece of earth. I didn't want to look at the dead, but I knew I had to, just as a criminal has to return to the scene of the crime. I couldn't help myself. I wanted to understand how it felt to be dead. The sounds of last night must be connected to something. Maybe it was to the afterlife. Would it be dark too? Or would there be white light and peaceful sounds?

Maybe the old saying "Rest in Peace" was a good one. God help them if they were not really resting in peace and quiet. I knew that if I were wasted, I just wanted to rest and sleep, sleep and rest. If death was just the beginning, and the streets were really gold, it had to be better than this green, miserable place. It just had to be. And it didn't seem that hell could be much worse.

My estrangement from myself also allowed me to understand my fears. I wasn't afraid of death; I was afraid of dying in this place. Here the noise of death was overwhelming. There was no silent, peaceful slipping away of life. Passing was brutal and loud at first, then silent, then loud again, as more noise crawled into the ear. Then came the deafening sound of silence, as dead men began their eternal, noteless songs.

Still looking at the bags, I felt a sudden pang of sadness for the families that would soon learn of the death of their loved ones. They would have to struggle with their loss, as would the living wounded. I didn't worry about the fallen. Their battles were over. The dead had nothing left to struggle for.

After the dead and wounded were flown out, I went to see the damage of last night's noise of death. I approached a pile of rubble and saw pools of blood staining the dirt. The blood had a sweet-sick smell, just the right smell to attract the flies, and they were already feasting. A flash of anger hit me. It was obscene to go to war and have the flies feast on the blood of the knights in grungy armor. I wished it would snow and purify the landscape. Snow covers what man has done. It would cover these pools of blood, and when it melted, it would carry the blood into the earth. Dust to dust, blood to mud.

As I walked back to my dirt dog hole, I adjourned this meeting with the morbid, and the peculiar motion returned to normal.

The rumor mill spread the word that a five-hundred-pound bomb had hit us. The official word was that a friendly jet had jettisoned its bomb so it could land in Da Nang. (Whoever invented the term "friendly fire" must have gone to college.) The unofficial word was that a MiG fighter had slipped out of North Vietnam and made its hit on us. I guess it really didn't matter who had it right. Either by accident or design, seven Marines had been killed and many more seriously wounded. It had been a ghastly night.

By then I'd learned that just when you think you've lived the longest, darkest night, a longer, darker one will take its place. On day four the situation continued to deteriorate. The NVA had us plotted and began to hit us with mortars and rockets. We lived in dirt surrounded by the lush green forest, and our perimeter stood out like the edge of mole on a beautiful lady's face. We were easy targets for any dummy with a mortar tube. We heard "Incoming!" more and more, and every day we would lose two or three Marines to the flesh-carving shrapnel.

William had a friend down the line on the perimeter. These two were tight, and William would go down to his friend's bunker for a visit almost every day. On day six, his friend was moving out with his squad for a patrol. The manglers came down on the squad with precision, and some of the men were caught in the open and hit.

William got word that his friend had been hit—and hit bad.

With a grim face, he told me his friend had been all but castrated by the incoming.

"I hope they can fix him," he said. "He loved his women, and this will be more than he can take."

He kicked at the dirt and walked off to be alone.

I think most of us understood that arms and legs could, and would, be lost in this war, but until then I hadn't given much thought to losing that part of my body. It was something a teenager with high levels of testosterone did not want to think about. It was dangerous to think.

Life at the Washout continued to be snuffed out. More and more incoming pounded us without any real pattern. About the time you started to relax and began thinking about how dirty you were or how lousy the chow was, the rounds would slam in, interrupting your little pity party.

Sometimes I could hear the tubes pop. The high-pitched whistle followed. If you weren't by your hole, you had better find one quick. All you could do was hunker as close to the bowels of mother earth as possible and send up a flurry of prayers for protection. Each day we would lose more men to the cutting iron of the incoming manglers. Each day our numbers dwindled.

With each passing day, the war did its dirty work. The heat, the rain, the noise of agony, the silence of the dead—all of it worked to harden the spiritual core of my being. I had been raised as a God-fearing Christian. I still believed in God and knew I had been born again, but this new life seemed to have no relation to anything I'd been taught. The connections were coming loose, the estrangement becoming more radical. I wasn't angry about it—I was just numb—and I was changing into someone I didn't know. It's common to hear about the 1000-yard stare of combat veterans. I think many of us were approaching the 800-yard mark.

The hardening of one's heart and soul happens without fanfare. There is no bar mitzvah. The body bags lined up for transport bothered me less and less. Now it was "better them than me." I no longer wondered what it was like to be dead; I simply didn't want to be dead. The incoming caused moments of deep anxiety, but when it stopped, the relief of having survived was almost a cheap high. We joked about how close or how far the rounds had come to our personal little pits.

My mind and soul were wandering off the narrow road. I would cuss one moment and pray like a devout believer the next. If I felt safe, I was as irreverent as a drunken sailor; if I was hunkering against the manglers, I was as pious as a deacon. I recognized the inconsistency in my attitudes, and at times I would argue with myself. I carried a New Testament in my pocket, but I couldn't read it. Nothing I'd known was the same in this place; everything I thought I would be, I was not. I was losing myself to some dimension that I didn't understand—and now I wanted to spill some blood.

I wasn't alone. It was in the air. Lots of the guys were spoiling for a fight.

I was no general, but it seemed to me we were getting driven into the wood by hammer blows that showed no signs of letting up. Grunts in foxholes don't worry much about tactics. Grunts are told to go, and grunts go. But to this lowly private, it seemed as if we were a covey of quail that got ourselves ground-sluiced almost every day. If this bird had had wings, I would have flown over the jungle and found the little yellow men throwing manglers at us. Then I would have dropped a load of bird poop on them as spotter rounds for our big guns.

When you ask young men to take blows from the enemy without shooting back, you're damming up a lot of potential energy that can go kinetic in a flash, and as the days wore on, tempers began to flare. We were tired of letting the enemy do all the slugging while we did all the ducking. We didn't want to keep sitting in the dog dirt getting sliced and cut by the manglers. We wanted to fight.

5
FATAL TERRAIN

Once in a while, we got a chance to get out of the Washout, usually on deployments called "reactionaries." They were, as our gunnery sergeant put it, "one hell of a way to make a living."

On one reactionary, a company of Marines ran into some stubborn NVA to our west, and we were sent to help. We were in a big hurry to get to the company in the fight, but as we approached it, the manglers came rolling in at us. There wasn't any cover, and one volley caught me in the open with no place to go. I saw an old fighting hole and launched myself into the air in a flying attempt to get inside the hole before the mangler hit. Midair, I was disappointed to find that two Marines had already arrived. I tried to change my direction of flight, but Marine grunts don't fly very well, and I crash-landed. I covered my head with my hands and hoped for the best. The round exploded close enough to raise my prostrate body off the earth.

The smell of burning iron mixed with an odor I thought was my flesh. I was afraid to look. Instead, I looked up at the two wide-eyed faces staring down at me.

"Damn, that was close," one of the faces said in a shaky voice.

I closed one eye to look at the damage. I didn't think I could bear to see my wounds with both eyes open. Steam kept spewing up into my face, but I felt no pain. That was good. At least I wouldn't be screaming and moaning. I hated the noises of the wounded, and I didn't want to add my own agonized cries to the din.

The foot-long, jagged piece of red-hot pig iron had come to rest just under my armpit. One more inch and it would have torn my arm off. I looked up at the two faces.

"Thanks for saving me a spot in the hole," I said.

"Hey, man," one face replied, "first come, first serve."

"Yeah," said the other face. "Where'd you learn to fly, anyway?"

"Hey, my take-off was perfect," I said. "I just couldn't stay in the air. It's hard to defy gravity when you're dressed like a turtle and carrying more weight than a pack mule."

I was adapting. I could smile even when the water ran down my leg.

Another mangler hit, then another, slam dancing up the line. A corpsman was called, and I thanked God once again for sparing me a bloody mangling or a noisy death.

We made our way up a small knoll. Marines were dug in, firing small arms almost casually. One Marine had sustained a head wound and was sitting in his foxhole with no helmet on. A thick compress was wrapped around his head, and he was weeping and wailing. I don't know if he was in pain or shock or both. From what I could see, his wound didn't seem serious, but he was almost out of control. His wails grated on my nerves.

Everyone was looking down the other side of the hill for any sign of enemy heading our way, and they ignored him. My squad also ignored him as we passed by his pit, but for some reason I had to look at him, and our eyes met. His were full of tears, and to him mine probably looked lifeless. I had no expression of compassion to give him, no sign that I felt his pain—just a look that passed from my eyes to his that said nothing.

The Marine carried on until someone with a voice of authority finally hollered, "Shut the hell up!" I looked over my shoulder to see how the wounded man would react. He slunk down into the hole and became quiet. A hard-looking Marine sitting close to him just shook his head.

A burst of enemy fire rattled off in the distance. We all ducked. One Marine commented that the gook had been shooting on and off all day and couldn't hit shit. I wondered how he knew it was the same person, but I didn't bother to ask. As far as I was concerned, it was never a wasted motion to duck at incoming fire. I'd heard it said that you never hear the one that hits you. I didn't want it to be said that I should have ducked.

At dusk we dug in and prepared for a counterattack. I was tense with anticipation, but, other than that, it wasn't a bad night. I was too tired to feel much fear, and it was almost a relief to be away from the Washout. For once the weather was bearable, and the bugs must have been on vacation. Spooky flew over a couple of times and entertained us with a light show as it spewed tracers into the night sky. I wondered what it was like to fight a war from the sky. It had to be better than humping, sweating, and spending the night in holes made for foxes.

Off in the distance, the rumble of bombs made their own night noise. This was not a light strike. A very heavy concentration of bombs exploded one after the other, making the earth shudder. The vibrating was eerie. Having survived one bomb, I understood the terror our bombs could deliver to our enemies. It was easy to imagine them enduring their own night of torment. I wished I could hear their screams.

Even as I asked God to forgive me, I hoped that many of them were dying tonight and that those who lived would have their ears full of their comrades' cries of pain and agony. It was good for my demented soul to know that the enemy was finally suffering in its own bloody hell. I hoped that there were many flies to feast on their blood. I hoped they were choking on the terror.

The next morning we headed back to the Washout. It hadn't been much of a fight. Apparently the enemy had engaged the Marines and then disengaged and disappeared into the thick forest before we arrived. Another day of hit and run, run and hit. We had been gone for less than twelve hours and had sustained a couple of wounded from the manglers. The outfit we had come to help had at least one killed and one wounded. We followed them off the hill, but I had no idea who they were or where they were headed.

As we marched, I saw a grunt carrying a dead Marine over his shoulder. At one point the dead man slipped off his comrade's shoulder and bounced on the ground. I had never heard a dead man hit the ground before. It sounded like a big chunk of soft rubber hitting semihard dirt. Another Marine offered to help with the load, but the packer waved him off. About that time our column veered off their trail to the right, and we continued our silent march back to the Washout.

I don't think many officers who commanded troops in the field had studied the history of the warfare of this little backward country. I know we ignorant grunts had no idea what we were up against. The manglers were doing exactly what these backwoods warriors wanted them to do. We didn't sleep, eat, or relieve ourselves without worrying about getting hit. It was gnaw at our flesh, devour our nervous system, and play with our brains.

One activity that was a study in terror was the night listening post, which was meant to provide an early warning if Charlie was sneaking about or making ready to attack. This assignment was usually handed to a squad, which would slip out beyond the wire and lie in the jungle all night. The old saying of being between a rock and a hard place was about the best description of your situation if you found yourself on a listening post. It could turn into a bloodbath if Charlie did come calling or if someone inside the perimeter had an itchy trigger finger.

Trick or treat, beat feet, don't sleep.

Outside the wire the yellow men were the deadly ghosts of the woods. Inside the wire the manglers and the special agents were our adversaries. The manglers were the most feared, but the special agents were also cause for alarm. They had four legs, long tails, and sharp, dirty teeth. Their eyes were slanted like those of our human foes, and they seemed to be expert commandos.

One night I was in my bunker tossing and turning, trying to sleep. I had just completed watch, and my eyes were heavy, but my body couldn't find a comfortable spot on the dirt floor of the bunker. Finally I nodded off. I was just about to enter a deep sleep when a ball of fur landed square on my face. It smelled like rotten bacteria and contaminated dirt, as if the thing had been down at the latrines for lunch. I was so disgusted and angry that I jumped up, cursing the stinking creature.

I'd forgotten about the low ceiling of the bunker, and I hit my head so hard that I actually saw stars. My head hurt so badly that I was forced to ignore the rat, which seized the opportunity to run down the full length of my body and fasten its grip my left leg. Holding my head, I finally shook it loose, but in the dark pit of the bunker I couldn't tell where the wretched thing was. It could have been sitting in a corner, just waiting for me to lie back down. I fixed bayonet and made ready for further battle. Poking and prodding, I attempted to locate it, but to no avail. I slept no more that night. In the morning light, the purple knot on my head was proof of the night's skirmish with the rat commando. I had a headache, and the rat was probably sleeping peacefully in the walls of the bunker.

If one of these agents bit a Marine, it wasn't all bad, because it meant seven days in the rear for rabies shots. Several Marines had gone through the treatment, and the only complaint they had was about the length of the needle. They had slept well for a week, a fact they rubbed in to those of us who were running low on rest.

Compared to rats, leeches were just nuisances. On day patrols it was very common to see the man in front of you with blood running from various parts of his body. Blood would seep through his clothing, or simply run down his arm or leg and become visible. The patrol would usually halt so the leeches could be assassinated with mosquito repellent. Every once in a while they would suck on a Marine who couldn't handle things eating his blood. When he freaked out, someone calmer would squirt the bug juice on the vampire. The blood-filled, worm-looking thing would fall off the Marine, and we would move out.

The days began to blur. Sleep was something we could only wish for. During the day we patrolled or worked on our foxholes and bunkers. We filled sandbag after sandbag and put them in what we hoped was just the right spot to stop the incoming. Our utilities began to cake up with red dirt and mud from living like wild dogs in our dens. If cleanliness truly is next to godliness, it might help explain part of the spiritual battle I was fighting. Our ancestral cavemen probably lived more sanitary lives than we did at the Washout.

Even though the rest of our bodies were beginning to itch and burn from the jungle rot, in good keeping with Marine tradition, we were forced to shave almost everyday. Our helmets became bowls to hold the water, and somehow the Marine supply line made sure we had enough razors to scrape off our peach fuzz. I often wondered why the generals found it so important to have us shave when most of us didn't even have an extra pair of socks.

Food was another problem. The C rations were becoming very dull. My mom had sent me a can of bacon, and one morning I decided to cook it. It was a big mistake. Everyone knows the smell of bacon. It reminds us of home—of comfort, of family, of good times. I didn't think about that when I opened the can of bacon. I just wanted something besides canned C rations.

When the aroma began drifting around thee perimeter, Marines I'd never seen before started to wander by to investigate. I did share with William, but it was difficult to enjoy the taste of the bacon under the longing looks of those who didn't get any. I wrote Mom and told her that the bacon was delicious but that it would be better if she didn't send any more. I didn't want to die at the hand of some Marine driven insane by the smell of bacon.

During all this, there were a couple of episodes that provided some comic relief.

No matter what one man tries to do to another, Mother Nature still controls the body. When it's time to go, it's time to go. One morning things were quiet, and a Marine slipped down to the latrines to answer the call. When the manglers came whistling in, they caught him with his pants down and squatting. He grabbed his pants and ran for cover.

Running with his pants partially up, the Marine fell. A round exploded nearby. After the dirt settled, he jumped up and began his mad dash again, the pants still causing him serious problems. From all appearances, the incoming had singled him out for today's mangling. His bare derriere was plainly visible as he ran, fell, got up, and ran again. A cheerleading squad began yelling and whistling in support of his bare-assed charge for cover. Each round came a little closer to our hero. Each time a mangler landed, we wondered if he had survived. We waited for the smoke to clear and for him to reappear. All in all, eight rounds chased the Marine in his pants-hung-low run.

After the attack someone yelled at the hard-breathing survivor, "Hey Marine, the job's not finished until you've done your paperwork!"

To make a point, sometimes it's more effective to use sign language than it is to use words. The Marine pulled up his pants, looked over at the comic, and gave him the universal sign of one finger sticking high in the air. The cheerleaders roared and clapped.

Another incident involved a pair of Marines nobody could quite figure out. They were inseparable, yet they fought almost constantly. If they weren't arguing and swearing at each other, they were pushing each other around. It was some kind of love-hate relationship.

One day we got word that a typhoon was on the way. We were told to brace for the storm as best we could. We were also told to man our positions around the perimeter and to keep our eyes open for any sign of enemy activity. It would be a good time for Charlie to come calling because low ceilings and high winds would keep us from getting air support. The storm came as advertised, and Marines in foxholes were rapidly flooded out. I was lucky: I'd been assigned watch from a bunker and had a roof over my head. Water was pouring in, but it wasn't running down my back, at least for the moment.

Over the barrel of my rifle I could see that the two buddies had abandoned their hole. They were huddled under a poncho, with the wind and horizontal rain beating against their little plastic fort. Every once in a while, a hand would appear out from under the poncho and attempt to hold it in place. Suddenly the poncho burst open, and one Marine whaled on the other with flying fists.

"What do you suppose that's all about?" I asked my partner.

He laughed. "I think someone fluffed."

It was the first and last time I heard William laugh.

The minislugfest lasted for about three blows, after which the two worked together to gather the poncho around their wet, soggy bodies. The storm passed, and we spent the rest of the day bailing out our holes and trying to get warm.

These instances of black humor may have given us some laughs, but the only true bright spot was mail call. A whole book could be written on the importance of mail call. A letter from home was the most important event of our degraded existence. It was our only link to the world we had left behind, a world that, with every passing day, seemed more and more like only a memory. Mail helped us keep our dreams. If you lose your dreams, you lose your mind.

My girl wrote almost every day. Sometimes the mail would not make it to us for a few days, but when it did there would be letters dated from one day to the next. I tried to return the favor, but some days when it was pouring rain or we were busy with patrols or construction, it was impossible. Whenever I did write, I tried to tell her how much her letters meant to me.

Not all mail was good, however. Bad mail always began with "Dear John," and it was easy to spot the guys who got it. Their already dull expressions became even duller, with darker shades of depressing gray on their lips. The wife of one guy asked for a divorce through the mail. Can you believe it? A mail-order divorce out here in the middle of this godforsaken piece of rotting landscape. The Marine tried to hide his pain, but his shoulders sagged, and he walked as if in a daze.

Here we were, the grungy, grunting guardsmen of freedom, and this guy's wife was cheating on him with some lowlife who was enjoying the comforts of his home. It was bad enough to hear news of protests in the streets, but to hear of disloyal lovers was worse. It was crushing mail, mail that should have been intercepted and burnt with the garbage. It was apparent that if every Marine received bad mail, it could wipe out an entire unit.

Fortunately there was plenty of good mail. Letters scented with a lady's favorite perfume would provide the addressee with many long, pleasurable inhalations. This simple act of pleasure produced many smiles and even a few loud whoops.

I was confident that I would never receive bad mail. My girl had promised.

About the third week into our trial by fire and water, I noticed a group of Marines moving toward our perimeter. Having nothing better to do, I sat on top of my bunker and counted them as they trudged by. They looked as dirty and tired as we did. After about thirty bodies, I saw a familiar face. I couldn't believe my eyes. There, looking me right in the eye, was Johnie Machau.

Johnie had graduated a year ahead of me. He was about the slipperiest halfback I'd ever seen. Football wasn't really my game, but I played for one season anyway. I'd seen Johnie outrun and outmaneuver many would-be tacklers. I did get a small piece of his uniform at one practice session, but that was as close as I ever came to bringing the guy down.

Now here he was, marching past the Washout. I raised my hand and waved, and he did the same. Neither of us spoke. Johnie disappeared off in the distance, and that was it. It was the last time I saw him. About a week later a letter from home told me that Johnie had been killed the day after I saw him. The war didn't care who he was or what he'd done. It didn't play favorites, and now Redmond had lost its second son.

We continued to get hit day and night. There was never one large assault, just enough manglers coming in to kill or maim one or two, and sometimes three or four. But the effect was just the same—the noise of feet running in the night to aid the wounded and dying, the moans of pain floating through the night air and hanging over it like a bad fog.

We sat and endured. We didn't talk much about the dead or the wounded. It was as if denying reality allowed us to keep hanging on. It was a tightrope act, and I don't think any of us knew how far the ground was from the rope. If we'd been sensitive to all the death and maiming, it surely would have dumped us off that rope. We would have been a gaggle of unstable Marines who wouldn't have been able to fight their way out of a paper bag.

At week four, Red and I had a conversation about our situation. Red always, and I mean always, had a radio to his ear or very close by. It had grafted itself to Red, and he to it. As radioman, he had direct contact with the company commander, and he confided to me that the CO was concerned about our dwindling numbers.

"How many of us are left?" I asked.

"We're down to less than half our original strength," he said.

Almost every morning we could hear the sounds of choppers coming to pick up the dead. It had become routine to see body bags ready for shipment. I don't know how many bags they had in inventory, but I figured if things didn't change pretty soon, we'd run out of Marines to put in them.

We were called out for another reactionary. Again a bunch of Marines were pinned down, and again we hustled to their position. My squad was ordered to advance to a tree line and eliminate several sources of fire. As we charged, a round exploded near my right ear. It sounded like a firecracker going off. There was no pain, but I quickly ran my hand along my face. There was no blood. A bullet must have sped past very close to my face.

I tried to run faster, but my charge was cut short. I didn't see the small crater that claimed my body. The pain in my left ankle was so bad that for a moment I thought I'd been shot in the leg, but I soon realized that I'd fallen into an old pungi pit. The good news was that there weren't any pungies in the pit; the bad news was that I'd sprained my ankle so severely that I could barely stand the pain. I felt light-headed and sick to my stomach.

Above the pit a fight was going on, and I was useless. For the first time in a long spell I had a chance to fight back, but now Charlie had once again used his ingenuity to remove one more Yank from the fighting. He hadn't spent a dime on the weapon that stopped me. I hit the wall of the pit with my fist. I was very angry to be taken out like that. I couldn't even fire my weapon for fear of hitting the men from my squad who were in front of me.

The small arms fire diminished, and a corpsman jogged past me. I hollered at him for help but told him I wasn't wounded. He said he had a couple of wounded up front and would be back for me as soon as he could. I gave him a thumbs-up and lay back in the hole. I felt like a real gomer for having been injured this way, but there was nothing I could do about it.

I was medivaced evacuated with a couple of Marines who had gunshot wounds. I tried to not show any pain. No one asked where I'd been hit, and I didn't say a word. I didn't want to divulge my injury. I hoped that I could get in and out of the field station without the wounded Marines knowing anything about it.

This was my first chopper ride, and I fell in love. Even with my ankle throbbing and the embarrassment I was feeling, I thought the helicopter was about the neatest thing since my old Chevy truck back home. I was free from the bonds of the earth. Right then and there I decided that I was going to learn to fly. Someday I would have wings that worked.

Looking down at Dong Ha, I had a flashback to the unfriendly reception I'd received the first time I landed there. Now I understood. It was the most forward rear area of the entire war, and incoming constantly harassed those who operated there. It was only slightly better than living in the bush, and it would make anyone cranky. I'd also learned that new guys were the worst of bad luck. It may have been superstition, but it did seem that new guys did in fact get wasted on a regular basis, and this wasting made old guys very nervous. New guys got old guys killed. It didn't matter if you were a handsome, poster-perfect Marine, or a pimple-faced stumblebum, you were new and therefore someone to be avoided.

We landed at Dong Ha. All of us were walking wounded, but I hobbled more than the others did because my ankle wouldn't support any weight. I made my way into the tent and found a chair. I sat down, extended my leg, and looked up. I wasn't prepared to see what lay on the gurney directly in front of me.

A human being lay there writhing in pain, burnt from head to toe. The head of the body had no facial features, and the torso looked like a roasted pig. I wanted to move away, but there were no other seats available. I tried not to stare, but I was like a spectator at a horror movie with a wraparound screen. There was no escaping the sight. To look down at my feet seemed a sign of disrespect for the person lying in charcoal in front of me. It was almost incomprehensible that no one was in attendance. The poor soul lay in solitude, dying alone. It seemed an unforgivable sin to let someone—anyone—die this way. There I sat with my sprained ankle, while just a few feet away was someone in a kind of pain that I couldn't even imagine.

A doctor appeared in front of me. He ignored the pitiful site. I must have been flushed with exasperation and nausea because the Doc looked at my face before he asked me what was wrong. I told him about the injury to my ankle, and he asked me to remove my boot. I hadn't unlaced it yet or even bothered to look at the damage. The boot came off with some pain, but if someone had been sawing off my leg, I don't think I would have even whimpered. My injury was absolutely nothing. All I wanted was to get treated and get the hell out of that so-called hospital. I'd almost bolted earlier, but I'd been in the Marines long enough to know that if I returned without a doctor's chit, I would be in serious trouble with my commanding officer.

The doc hastily wrote out a chit that called for light duty. My ankle had swelled to the size of a Texas grapefruit. The doc told me to stay in the rear for a few days and to keep ice on it. Then he had a corpsman wrap it with an ace bandage.

In the background the crispy body continued its slow, twisting dance. If the writhing stopped, the shaking began. I still couldn't believe my eyes. I thought maybe it was just a dream, but when the figure gasped for air and moaned, it seemed very real. No matter where I went, the noise of death seemed to follow.

As soon as the corpsman finished, I hobbled out of there as fast as my one good foot would allow. The outside air settled my nerves. I could swallow again without fear of throwing up. I had acquired a strong stomach in the last few weeks, but the sight of the burnt offering had pushed my limits. I said a speedy prayer for the miserable burn victim, asking God to have mercy and send the angel of death quickly. I had never before prayed for someone to die.

I made my way to battalion headquarters to report in. I limped and hobbled around other tents and through a sea of moving people. By the time I got near the headquarters tent, I had decided to find a chopper back to my unit. Although there would be no ice there, I knew that I had to get as far away from this place as fast as I could. Not only did I need to take my mind off the horror I had just witnessed, but those still left at the Washout needed the help of every man to protect our perimeter. I figured that if I went back to my unit, I could at least fill sandbags and take my turn standing watch. I didn't want to be known as a skater. I wasn't trying to be stupid; I just wanted to do my duty.

Somehow I found a chopper going straight to the Washout with a load of mail and ammo. I asked the door gunner if I could hop a ride, and he smiled and nodded. I climbed in and propped up my bad leg up to ease the throbbing. I hurt, but the hurt was almost causing me joy. I knew my ankle would heal, and for the first time in a long time, I knew I could face any incoming as long as it did not contain fire. That day I developed an intense dread of being burned—a fear that is with me to this day. Napalm will never smell good.

A strange thing happened the day after I returned to the Washout. I had gotten into a conversation with a corporal who was a squad leader in another platoon. He asked about my ankle, and I told him that it hurt less but that it was still painful to walk much.

"Well," he said, "each squad has its cull." Then he walked off.

I was livid. Right then I could have been in Dong Ha whining about how I couldn't return to duty. I could have milked that ankle for the rest of the war.

William happened to walk by and saw me shaking in anger.

"What's going on?" he said.

I told him what the corporal had said.

"Don't pay attention to that scumbag," he said. "Did you know he used to be a sergeant?"

I shook my head.

"He shot himself in the foot during a bad firefight and got himself a chopper ride out. Would have gotten away with it too, but one of the wounded on the chopper saw him do it and was pissed when they gave him a Purple Heart. He told the story to the captain, who had the sergeant court-martialed for cowardice under fire. Story is, the corporal won't be allowed to leave Nam until he is dead or an old man."

This story made me even madder. The bag of rat manure had just insulted the hell out of me. I started to limp after him. William grabbed my arm.

"Let it go. He'll get wasted one day, and that'll be the end of it."

I wanted a chunk of his hide, but I would listen to my partner. I did tell him to pass the word that the no-good S.O.B better never come near me again.

One day we got word that anyone interested in volunteering for a new company being formed was to let the captain know. It was a reconnaissance company. Not knowing exactly what these guys did, I consulted Red. He'd been in country for a long time and was getting short. I respected his knowledge and his opinions.

"Man you are crazy to think about going recon," he said.

"Why?"

"Those guys are nuts. They go out on eight-man patrols deep into Charlie country. Do you know how many of them don't get out alive? Do you know how many teams get wasted with no survivors?"

"Nope," I said. I had never heard about them.

"Besides, they won't take you with that bad ankle."

As far as my ankle was concerned, the swelling was diminishing daily, and I didn't think anyone had bothered to log it on my medical records.

Red continued his argument. "It's a lot safer to stay with a larger outfit," he said.

I listened intently, but the fact was that Charlie monitored every move we made at the Washout. I couldn't go to the bathroom without knowing that some Charlie was watching me with binoculars. And whenever we moved in the bush, we sounded like a herd of buffalo. It was easy for the enemy to know how many of us were coming and where we were going. Every time we tried to hunt them in the jungle, we paid a heavy price for invading their domain.

There is an ancient saying in the military: "Never volunteer for anything." Had that been leaked to civilians, I wouldn't even be considering it now. But I had passed on the chance to be in the Navy, as well as to dodge this entire affair, and had volunteered. Now I was trying to assess my options.

I told Red that I'd think about it and get back to him before dark.

Not so long ago, I'd been a happy-go-lucky teen who found it a strain to have to sit down and think something through. I lived on impulse. If it was a warm, sunny spring day, I was apt to skip school and go fishing. If Dad had a good bull on the ranch, I was apt to throw a rope on him and see which of us was the better. But that was before life as a Marine. Now here I sat, dirty, tired, and sensing that my role in this little perimeter was nothing more than a part of some big plan that I had absolutely no understanding of. Looking around at our little wired-in fort, I thought about my chances of survival if I stayed. It came down to this: Things couldn't be any worse.

I walked back up to Red's bunker and told him to tell the captain I would be delighted to volunteer for recon.

The next day I was told to gather my stuff and be ready to catch a chopper out of the Washout. A flood of relief washed over my soul. I wanted to laugh and cry at the same time. But when the chopper landed, I was standing alone, and second thoughts rippled through me. *Was I the only one who said he would go? Did everyone else know something I didn't?* I thought about lowering my raised hand. I was feeling like a kid in school who had decided he didn't need to go the bathroom after all.

The door gunner motioned me to hurry up and get aboard. The manglers could come at any time. The chopper lifted off and I waved good-bye to Red. He didn't return the wave. He just shook his head and looked down at the ground.

The fatal terrain of the Washout became smaller and smaller.

C. W. Standiford

PART II
SWIFT, SILENT, DEADLY

*War is war, hell is hell,
and the two become one
when one man lives to kill another.*

6
ECHO COMPANY

The chopper landed at Phu Bai. I found the headquarters tent for the Third Battalion and took a minute to study its logo. The words *swift, silent, deadly* formed an arch over a skull and crossbones. It amused me. I didn't mean to belittle my former outfit, but we'd been more dead than deadly.

I had no idea what I was heading into, but when the office warrior gave me directions to the showers, I figured that whatever the future held, it would be worth it just to get a hot shower and some clean clothes. I must have smelled like a latrine, because the guy kept his distance while he talked to me.

It had been more than forty days since I'd had a real bath. We'd gone to the river once to rinse off, but I don't remember a bar of soap ever hitting our scaly skins. As I headed to the showers, other grunts came wandering in. I don't know what outfits they came from, but they looked and smelled just like I did. It was good to know that other knights of grunge had been out there living like alley dogs.

I could have stayed in the shower until my tour was up. The shower room had three stalls, and from the moans of pleasure I heard, I wasn't the only one who found the clean, soapy water almost heaven. There is something renewing about having a clean body. When the body is filthy, the soul tends to follow. This water could break Satan's spell. It flushed my soul as well as my body, and I began to feel purified.

The clean utilities felt like expensive Chinese silk on my new skin. The new socks felt like soft lamb's wool. I chuckled to see pairs of new skivvies piling up. Apparently the supply guys still thought we didn't leave home without them. I wouldn't trade in my boots, though. Even though I felt clean and new, there was no way I would discard my old boots. I had to hang onto something old to prove I wasn't new.

The brand-new feeling lasted about twenty minutes. The hot, humid air rapidly sucked the freshness out of everything, and I began to sweat. At least it was a clean sweat—that is, it started out as a clean sweat. The dirt must have worked deep into my pores, because soon I started to feel dirty again.

The next order of business was food. Thinking that any meal that wasn't C rations would top off the blessed events of the day, I made my way to the mess hall. Whatever they plopped on the plate from my mess kit looked about as appetizing as a dead fish with its eyes staring up at me, but I ate it anyway. As I ate, I watched and listened to the Marines who were coming and going from the mess tent. It was easy to spot the bush hogs. A couple of Marines sat down next to me.

"You part of Third Recon?" one of them asked.

I nodded. "Just got here. I'm waiting for formation at 1600. You too?"

The other Marine nodded. "I hear we're going to Okinawa for training," he said. "We get out of Nam for six weeks!" There was wild excitement in his voice.

Six weeks in Okinawa. I couldn't believe what I heard. A person cannot be in two places at once, so if we went to Oki, it obviously meant that we wouldn't be here.

At the formation we were introduced to Captain Raymond, our new commanding officer. He broke the news: We would fly out of this mad maze in the morning and go to Okinawa for six weeks of recon training. Six weeks of no manglers. Six weeks of no nights in the jungle. Six weeks of playing war with no real bullets. We all smiled like little boys who had just received BB guns for Christmas.

Things were looking so good that I thought maybe I was in a dreamworld. I'd had a hot shower and some decent conversation with other volunteers, and we were getting out of here for a stint. We'd been given free time for the evening. We didn't have to fill sandbags or stand watch. We even got to sleep in tents with floors—on cots! If only Red could see and hear all this. Tonight I would take one more shower, write my family and my girl, and then sleep as I hadn't slept in more than fifty days. If I died in my sleep, I would die in grunt comfort.

In the morning we boarded a C-130 and flew out of Vietnam. The drone of the engines almost hypnotized me. I was so relaxed that I couldn't keep my eyes open, and I slept until the props reversed on the Okinawa airstrip and jolted me forward. We got off the plane and were bussed to some very nice barracks. The first thing I noticed was the cooler air. I could breathe without drawing a sweat.

There was a formation at 1100, and after roll call we were marched to the mess hall. The smell of food hit my nose and made my stomach growl. I breathed in the aroma of hot coffee. I was more than ready for a decent meal. The food was fit for royalty, and the coffee tasted as good as it smelled. So far this volunteerism was paying off.

After we ate, we went outside so some of the guys could have a smoke before the next formation. We introduced ourselves and began making friends. We swapped war stories and talked about our grunt units and where we'd been in Nam. A few of the guys had received orders from stateside units and were assigned to Third Recon when they landed in Nam. This new company would be a mix of "old" bush hogs and some new guys fresh from the States.

When everyone had finished eating, we met in the building across from the chow hall. There were nearly a hundred of us. We were called to attention, and a first lieutenant dressed in really cool camouflage entered the room and stepped up on the stage.

"At ease!" The lieutenant looked around the room.

He smiled. "Welcome to Echo Company, Third Recon."

A smiling officer? *Ha!* I figured I was about to learn that I'd really screwed myself. I was still wondering why more of my grunt company comrades hadn't raised their hand to volunteer. Now I would find out what Red had been trying to tell me.

"Gentlemen, you have become part of a unit that will be the eyes and ears for the Third Marine Division." The lieutenant kept smiling as he spoke. "You soon will become the tip of the spear."

The lieutenant went on to tell us what we would be doing for the next six weeks. We would learn how to read a map and compass and how to call in air and artillery support. We would be taught how to wage war in the jungle, how to make water assaults in rubber rafts, how to rappel off cliffs and out of choppers—and a host of other war-making skills.

He stated more than once that we would learn to operate as a team and become a cohesive unit that would be swift, silent, and deadly. This approach to warfare made very good sense to me, and as I listened, I actually became excited. From the sound of things, I would never again be a sitting duck in some mud hole. Even so, the stark reality was that there would be plenty of opportunities to die in other ways. The lieutenant made that very clear.

"Marines, the work you will be doing is dangerous and at times lonely. You will be operating in small teams of six to ten Marines. You will be inserted deep into Charlie country, and your survival will depend on stealth, discipline, and skill. Just recently we lost an entire team in a fierce fight. The Marines fought bravely, as Marines do, but there were no survivors. We recovered the bodies, and I must tell you that from the scene of the battle, Charlie paid a high price for picking a fight with that little band of Marines."

The difference between being a line grunt and a recon Marine was becoming apparent. The lieutenant's story confirmed what Red had said: A small band of Marines could easily become targets of predators. It would be like getting into the water where a large number of man-eating sharks were waiting to feast on our flesh.

The room was stone silent. The lieutenant let the silence make his point, and it hit home like a freight train going the wrong way in a one-way tunnel. Those of us who had been grunts had seen death. Our new jobs could mean that an entire small team could be wasted out there in the hostile jungle.

For me, it was a lonely thought. I had always imagined that someday there'd be one big, bloody fight—a fight where we would go in, root out the enemy, and take his real estate. That's how Marines had done it here at

Bury Me With Soldiers

Okinawa, at Guadalcanal, at Iwo Jima, and in almost every battle the Marines had ever fought. I can still remember when someone at the Washout said that we were going to invade North Vietnam and put an end to the war. It was probably the best rumor I'd ever heard. The mood was one of elation. I believe every soul in that company would have chosen to fight a major conflict rather than endure a slow mangling.

After we chewed on the lieutenant's words for a while, he went on to tell us how important our work would be. The division needed information on enemy movements and strongholds. Our mission was not to engage the enemy, but to find them, count them, and bring that information back to division intelligence. There would be times, we were told, that we would be asked to capture prisoners or harass the enemy with ambushes or artillery and air strikes, but by and large, we were to avoid contact unless we knew we had the upper hand.

The meeting ended with the lieutenant passing out our training schedule to the platoon commanders. These were a mix of second lieutenants and a few staff and gunnery sergeants. We were told to go outside and stand in formation so we could be assigned to our teams. The new terminology was refreshing. Squads had become teams; patrols were now missions.

At 0500 the next morning we were running and singing. One thing has never changed about the United States Marine Corps: If someone isn't trying to kill you and there are more than five unoccupied Marines in a cluster, you run and sing. I couldn't carry a tune in a bucket, but I enjoyed the chants that some demented Marines had composed just for running.

After the run we grabbed some chow and then went to the classroom. We studied the maps and compass every morning and then after lunch went into the field to practice what we'd learned. Each team member was expected to become an expert on every topic we covered. This was a lot different than the way grunts did things. In the grunts, you just saddled up and followed the Marine in front of you. No one, except the captain and maybe the platoon commanders, knew where we were headed and what we were going to do when we got there. In Okinawa, we learned to work as a chain with every link pulling the next. Live or die, I knew I had made the right decision in joining this outfit.

Even at the ripe old age of 19, I could see that the grunt wars would never resolve the permanent ownership of certain pieces of real estate. War at the Washout had been like a revolving door. It had been occupied before we got there, and someone had decided that it should be occupied again. We had lost over sixty Marines to wounds and death, and during all that time, I hadn't personally engaged the enemy. As a matter of fact, I hadn't even seen the enemy. I had endured his assaults and seen good men get wasted. We lived with one foot in the grave, and not once did it look like our feet would find a safer place anytime soon.

After a couple of weeks of classroom and afternoon fieldwork, we stuffed the all-too-familiar C rations into our packs and went camping and hiking for a few days. In the hills of Oki we played hide-and-seek with the other teams. We had briefings, read our maps for location fixes, set up ambushes, called in mock artillery, and even hid from aircraft flying over our locations.

In the briefing, the teams were shown their recon zones. The RZ was usually six square clicks on the map, or 6,000 square meters. A typical mission would require the team to scour and watch for enemy movements in the assigned area. Anything known about the enemy was disclosed during the briefing. The typical term used would be "contested," which meant that the enemy was probably there or had a history of being there. Other information included the weather forecast, the terrain, water availability, mode of insertion, available artillery support, and the proposed extraction date and site.

I was impressed with the briefing process. For the first time, I would go into the bush knowing something about the reason for our mission and what we would face. I would even know the names of every Marine I would be with. Once again I congratulated myself on my decision to join this band of painted faces.

One thing they hammered into us during training was the procedure for insertion by helicopter. The noise of the flying machine told anyone with ears that Americans had landed. We were told to get away from the landing zone as quickly as possible. It was bad practice to set up close to the LZ because Charlie knew right where to start prodding. Better to disappear into the bush and make it more difficult for the little buggers to seek and destroy. Ignoring this basic rule of operation had proven to be a potentially deadly omission of good operating procedure.

We wore no flack jackets or helmets in recon, and I felt like a spring colt bounding in the tall grass. The absence of that turtle gear was a giant relief. I know those two pieces of body armor saved many lives, but for me, they were miserable pieces of war equipment. I wouldn't have made a good knight, with my full-body armor clanking and banging and causing me to sweat profusely. I'd rather be comfortable in my discomfort than a walking piece of sheet metal. I agreed with the old warrior Sitting Bull, who said that only the rocks live forever. Even though I wasn't in any hurry to go exploring the afterworld, shedding the helmet and flack jacket made this life a happier place.

Sergeant Johnson started me off as point man. I made a terrible point. My ankle kept turning, and it made me stumble. So far I'd been able to hide the problem with my ankle from the entire outfit. The darn thing would be fine one day and useless the next. When you're on point, your eyes must do most of the work, and the feet must graciously follow. My feet were less than gracious. All it took was one little pebble or root on the trail to make me look like a clumsy oaf. Not wanting to leave the point position, I hung in there until the sergeant got tired of watching me hobble and big-foot around. He quietly moved me to rear guard, where no one could see me when I had trouble, and I was able to conceal my problem for the rest of the training.

After the third day in the bush, disaster hit our company. We were operating in swampy forest that had some dangerous bogs in and around the trees. One of the radiomen fell into one of them, and for some reason he couldn't be rescued. The details are foggy, but the heavy radio and field pack probably sucked him in so quickly that there was no way to find him under the dark green water. The accident brought home the fact that ours was a dangerous occupation and that none of us should ever be surprised when death knocked at one of our doors.

After the drowning of the radioman, it struck me again that here we were, very young men who had for one reason or another ended up packing weapons, fighting, and watching our countrymen get maimed and killed. Death even followed us as we trained to deliver death. Even so, we were able to protect ourselves from its sting. Something in our young minds seemed to block ordinary grief, like a water pump that seizes up and doesn't get the water out of the well. After each incident, we just went about our business. We had become experts of denial.

During training, our team got to know one another pretty well. Even though I didn't yet have a real basis for my opinion, I felt we were one of the best teams in Echo Company.

Sergeant Steve Johnson, our team leader, had come from another recon company and seemed to have quite a bit of experience.

Rudd and Greene were two African-Americans who appeared to be close friends. Everything was good between them and between them and the rest of us. They seemed steady, reliable Marines who would skillfully do whatever needed to be done.

Sergeant reminded me of the actor William Holden. I think it was his eyes. Sergeant was his real last name, and we had some good fun with that.

James McAfee, aka Mac, the skinniest and crankiest of the bunch, was the type who would spit in the wind and curse if it missed him.

Bruce Tuthill (aka Tut) was the boldest and brashest—the kind of Marine who would walk up to the Lone Ranger and pull off his mask. I learned that Tut hadn't volunteered for the Marines. He'd been given a choice: Go into the Marines or go to jail. He had gotten himself mixed up with some unruly folks, and the judge thought it would be better for the country if Tut went to Vietnam instead of wasting everyone's time and money sitting around in jail. Tut had this cocky smile that showed up every time there was a controversy or a fight in the bush. He would gently throw his head back and produce a happy little expression of defiance.

Tut was a very interesting character. Many times I would have liked to have crawled into his mind and inspected his gears. He and I would talk religion from time to time. I still held to my belief in God and a better world to come, while Tut had a strong agnostic point of view. At times when we argued, I thought I was making progress, but then he would counter with some point that left me stranded. I think we debated this subject off and on the entire time we were together. I can still remember lying in the dark tent just before we drifted off to sleep, arguing about the existence of God and life after death. The rest of the team always remained quiet during these friendly exchanges. They must have considered this running disagreement their nightly bedtime story.

One day Tut showed me his battle scars from the streets of Rhode Island. Someone had taken a can opener to his back, and the scar was a strong indication that when you want to fight, any sharp object can produce bodily harm. I saw Tut in a couple of altercations during training at Okinawa, and he always surprised his opponents with his ability to have them on the ground before they knew what had happened. I made a mental note to let Tut handle any hand-to-hand combat in the bush. I would have no problem being his water boy, waiting in the corner while he did battle with the little yellow men. As the days moved on, I gained more and more confidence in Tut. I came to appreciate his combat savvy and even his cocky attitude.

Tut liked to give us nicknames. His name for me would strike terror into the hearts and minds of the enemy. Other Marines would step aside when I walked down the company street. My name would go before me into the jungle, into the night. This name inspired so much terror that I could barely repeat it myself. My new name was Fudd, Elmer Fudd.

I don't know if Tut got this idea for the name because I reminded him of the cartoon character running around in the woods with a weapon chasing the "cwazy wabbit," or if it was because of my big ears and broad forehead. I never asked why, but I did ask him if Rocky, or Gunner, or even Maggot might not have been more suitable.

Tut just smiled that smile, and the name stuck.

All was well with the name changes. I didn't mind, and neither did Donald Schleman, whose nickname was Meatball. He was one of those guys everyone took an instant liking to. His down-home sense of humor and easygoing attitude made him fun to be around. If you didn't like this guy, you wouldn't like the rest of us.

Mail call for Meatball often consisted of a fishing report from the folks back home. Fishing appeared to be more than a hobby for the Schleman clan, and I know Meatball dearly missed his time on the water with his family. Many times he'd go around camp and show off pictures of the lunkers his family had caught. None of us would have been surprised to see him sitting next to a stream in the bush wetting a line. That would have made a picture to send home—a spinning rod in one hand and a weapon in the other. Maybe Meatball would have told his family that the fish in Vietnam were just too big to land unless he blew them into smaller pieces.

Our nicknames kind of made us stand out, and I'm certain the jungle drums warned the NVA that we were two of the baddest Marines around. I could just imagine Charlie sitting around camp swapping tall tales about two American teenage Marines named Fudd and Meatball. I'm certain they shook in their sandals.

Besides Tut, the other Marine who made me feel confident was Ernie Cooke III, a hulk who packed the radio as if it were weightless. He was the biggest and strongest of the group and had a steady-as-you-go attitude. Although Ernie hadn't been in combat yet, I didn't see any reason to treat him like a new guy. The new-guy syndrome didn't exist in this team. In fact, I don't think it existed in the entire company. We had gotten to know one another, and there was no reason to act aloof or worry that those who hadn't seen combat were bad luck for those of us who had.

One day Ernie and I got into some horseplay. We were building a wall of sandbags around our team tent, and we were about to finish that part of the project when we began our skirmish. We were filling and stacking the sandbags, and one of us did something to the other that set things off. I don't know why I thought I could throw Ernie to the ground, but for some reason I decided to attack and put that big boy on his back.

When Ernie's arms grabbed my body, I knew I'd made a huge mistake. I flew through the air, clearing the four-foot high sandbag wall. As a grunt, I had attempted to fly and had crash-landed. Now, catapulted by Ernie's strong arms, I flew quite well. By the time I hit the ground, I'd learned another lesson: If you want to fly, take a chopper.

After that incident, I figured that Ernie could throw the little yellow men at Tut, and Tut could stomp them into the ground. I could sit back in the shade, and when they were finished, I could hand them a drink of lukewarm canteen water while I critiqued their performance. As their self-appointed manager, I'd make sure they stayed healthy so they could always be in front of me when the yellow men came charging with quiet steel or flailing fists.

It would have been interesting to do a psychological profile on our little band. I believe that each of us had raised our hand for this duty, and, although I knew why I had volunteered, it would have been interesting to know why the others had. Maybe it was as simple as Ernie's explanation: He was waiting assignment after his arrival to Vietnam and someone asked him if he wanted to go to recon. Ernie's uncomplicated reply was "Hell, yes." Not "Hell, yes!" Just a simple, "Hell, yes."

Whatever it was, there was something about this group that gave me confidence. After only a few weeks of training, I knew each one of them a whole lot better than any of the grunts I'd been with at the Washout. There was a different attitude in this pack. Laughter wasn't hard to come by, and there was no 800-yard stare.

Mail call was still one of the most important events of our daily lives. But something in my girl's letters was different. I couldn't put my finger on it, but her words seemed more distant. I hoped that absence was making the heart grow fonder, not making her eyes wander. I really didn't want any bad mail.

I had remained true to her. On liberty in Oki, I was kidded because I didn't get into heavy drinking or involved with the fast ladies. I was engaged, and that meant I had promised myself to Sally. I could end up dying a virgin—a horrible thought—but I had my honor to uphold. I would save myself for her, even if my honor made me explode. It would be an ugly scene: A 19-year-old blows up from the inside out, all because Mother Nature had given him an overdose of male hormones.

I remembered something we learned in science class about the balance of nature. Whoever studied that subject had never been around scores of young healthy Marines far from home and with serious concerns about dying chaste. This caused a very serious, almost deadly, imbalance of nature. I fought the imbalance and remained faithful to my betrothed. I hoped she was doing the same. She just had to be doing the same.

Most of us are afraid of something—*really* afraid of it. Some are afraid of dark rooms; some come unglued at the sight of a little brown mouse. Me, I'm afraid of heights. My dad once told me that he put me on a coffee table when I was about two, and I threw a fit. When it comes to heights, you could call me a coward, and I would agree with you. If it were up to me, there wouldn't be a single building over twenty feet high, and instead of bridges over water, there'd be tunnels under water. Height can lock up my entire nervous system. All this to say that during training I had to face my biggest fear and that I did my darndest to sidestep the encounter.

We were trucked out to some very high, jagged cliffs for a training session in rappelling. I walked over to the edge of the cliff, looked down, and immediately became dizzy. All my life I'd had this dream where I was flying around in the sky and couldn't get back down. It was a weird dream, and sometimes I would wake up in a cold sweat. For a long time the dream came back at least once a week. As I looked down the cliffs, it was as if I had been here before. Maybe there was something to weird dreams. Maybe today I would live the dream; maybe I'd get airborne and not get back down. This was not a good day to die, and I wished I were a rock, not a Marine about to go down these vertical cliffs. I felt queasy.

The instructor spoke with extreme confidence as he showed us how to use the Swiss seat and D ring and how to use our gloved hand to brake our descent. I couldn't believe they expected me to trust my health and welfare to that thin piece of metal and a flimsy rope. What if the jagged rocks cut the rope and sent me hurtling down the cliff? In my mind I saw a freeze-frame of my battered body lying next to the rolling waves of the ocean. There would be no glory in dying on this beach. That glory had already gone to the Marines who captured this island from the Japanese during WWII. I didn't think they would name a base after me if I got splattered from a free-fall down the face of these rocks.

The instructor told us to form three lines. We would be fitted with our little rope seat and then bail off the cliffs in groups of three. I immediately went to the back of the longest line. Maybe a freak storm would show up and cancel this maniacal activity, or, if I hung to the rear, maybe no one would notice that I was still there.

The rest of the company seemed ready to step backwards off the cliff and enjoy the ride to the bottom. I must have been the only one there who felt nauseated and shaky. After each man disappeared over the cliff, the line advanced, bringing me closer to facing the worst fear of my life.

Suddenly there was a commotion on the middle rope. The instructor lay down on his stomach and peered over the cliff.

"What's the problem, Marine?"

"The D ring broke!" The Marine looked up for words of advice and encouragement.

"Use both hands and let yourself down slowly!" the instructor yelled.

I knew it! If God had wanted man to scale down these rocks, we would have been born with suction cups on our feet and hands.

Clutching the rope, the Marine carefully picked his way down the cliff, and the incident ended with no bodily injuries.

It was coming closer to the time when I'd have to go over the cliff. Attempting to avoid eye contact with the instructor of my line was not working. The guy must have sensed that I wasn't the least bit interested. I would rather have been challenged to bite the head off a chicken and chew on its brains than take one more step towards the cliffs. Finally, there was no one in front of me except the instructor. I had no one to hide behind and no place to go. There I stood, out in the open where the instructor could see every shade of green I was turning.

"Marine!" he bellowed.

Once again I wished I had wings that worked. I would flutter and float to the bottom of the cliff and land gently without the use of the rope. Oh, I wished for wings. Even suction cups would do.

The instructor's voice told me there would be no negotiating. Nothing was going to stop him from strapping me to the rope and seeing that I went over the precipice. Either I did it myself or he would throw me.

Leaning back against the rope, my eyes locked onto the instructor's eyes. His ugly face would be that last human image I'd see before I died. There would be no soft skin to feel, no pretty girl to gently hold my hand as I passed into the hereafter. The thought made me mad. I screamed at the top of my lungs something that was a cross between "God bless America!" and "Dear Jesus, I love you!"

The adrenaline flow was almost too much. I was afraid, but I was also slip-sliding my fear. The rope was holding my weight, and the only pain was that of the hot rope burning through my glove. I didn't even notice the ground below me. When my feet hit it, I suppressed my desire to let out a war whoop. I removed my Swiss seat and handed it to the instructor as if I had done this a hundred times. The instructor on the ground would never know the fear that had nearly consumed me at the top of those cliffs. As a matter of fact, this is the first time I have admitted to anyone how scared I really was.

I suppose I had better tell you now that there is one other thing I'm afraid of—snakes. It's difficult to be honest about your fears, especially when there are so many ways to die. It can make you appear to be weak. Maybe some strength comes when you know the fears and attempt to ignore them. Another mystery to be solved at another time. All I knew for certain was that a toe tag on my dead body with the word *snakebite* on it wouldn't be good. It would make me mad. I don't know if it's possible for a dead man to be mad, but if it is, dying from snakebite could do it. It would be no way to die, no way to suffer. The little reptile would suck the glory out of mortal combat. No one wants to die from snakebite. It's one of those inglorious ways to enter the kingdom of the dead.

One day as we were finishing up our training in Oki, our little group had a discussion. The subject was capture. We decided that we would fight to the last man and die before we waved the white flag. Maybe it was only brave talk, but I knew I didn't want to become a prisoner of the yellow men. More than once I'd dreamt of being bound and tortured, and I can tell you now, without fear of criticism, that I knew I wasn't man enough to uphold the code under torture. Other than the fear of heights and snakes, I couldn't imagine anything worse than having another man beat and torture me.

It would be my luck that they would suspend me over a cliff that had a large den of vipers at the bottom. I could imagine a little yellow man grinning as he cut one strand of the rope at a time. My eyes would bulge in fear, and I would spit in his face. That would bring a slap and another slash of the rope. I knew I was about to die, and the thought of falling into the snake pit turned me cold from the inside out. Would I die from fright as I fell, or would I die with a hundred snakes striking at my battered body? Or would my enemy show mercy and put a bullet in my brain before he cut the final strand of the rope. Not in this dream.

Sometimes it was difficult to sleep, and I wondered if the others ever thought about this crazy stuff. I knew that I wanted Tut and Ernie to save their last bullets for me. I wanted to die quickly at the hand of my fellow Marines, not at the hand of the enemy. I couldn't chance dishonoring the Marine Corps or myself.

Our training was just about complete. From swimming in the cold ocean to dangling out of choppers with a rope, I had stared down some of my fears and actually enjoyed the training. The cliff hanging had pushed me to the limit, but I'd done some things that were fun, too, and I felt equipped to go back and hunt for the enemy.

In fact, I was almost getting excited about returning to Nam. I wanted to put my new skills to the test. I wanted revenge for those who lay silent in the bags of doom, and I was ready to go back and do some serious payback. I wanted to see my enemy and cause him bodily harm. A dead Marine was a wasted Marine, but a dead Charlie was a good Charlie. I figured that once we ran out of Charlies, we could wrap up this war and go home. The nation would be grateful that we had done our job and stopped the communist threat to freedom around the world. So I thought.

God help Charlie if he crossed my path.

God help me if I crossed his.

God help us all.

7
CAT AND MOUSE

We returned to Vietnam in February 1968, ready to put our new skills to work. I don't remember hearing one complaint about going back to the war.

A C-130 transported us to our new base at Quang Tri. The C-130 is an airborne pack mule. It probably hauled more cargo—mail, ammo, food, people—than any other craft of the entire war. With four engines fighting the air, it could lift a full payload off a short field; by reversing props, it could land on the same short field. Of course you don't have good planes without exceptional people, and the pilots and crews who manhandled these planes had never given me cause for concern—until now. At the end of the runway at Quang Tri a wrecked C-130 sat in solitude. It appeared that the plane had run out of runway, spun around, and snapped off a wing. When our plane reversed props and threw us forward, I knew our pilot had maneuvered his craft skillfully. Turning the plane around at the end of the runway, he taxied it back so we could disembark.

We were given directions to our new company area. I was expecting bunkers and foxholes, so I was surprised to see a row of tents. Peering into one, I was further surprised to see cots and mosquito nets. I almost pinched myself. This was much better than a dirt floor inside a rat-infested bunker or dog hole.

There's an expression I used a lot in Vietnam: "hammered dog poop." I'm not sure, but I think I used it a lot because I'm the one who made it up. Anyway, somehow in my childhood I learned that if you take a hammer and hit a pile of dog poop, it flattens and splatters. At Quang Tri, I began to realize just how much the life a grunt at the Washout had resembled hammered dog poop. When new guys complained about the food, the heat, or anything, I didn't hesitate to tell them to go live with the line grunts for a spell. When they came back, they'd know just how good they had it in recon. Often they just looked at me and smiled, and I wanted to rub their smile in the dog poop. But we had no dogs.

One of the first things we noticed about Quang Tri was that there was no shortage of sand. While the mess cooks were cooking Spam for our first meal, we made jokes about fried Spam, boiled Spam, and baked Spam. You could add sand to the Spam simply by sitting in the tent and waiting for a breeze. The breeze would lift the sand and place it directly on the Spam. Spam 'n' sand would be our dietary mainstay until other supplies could be brought in. After a couple of meals of Spam 'n' sand, I went back to C rations. We thought maybe someday they'd make a movie about us and call it *The Spams of Quang Tri*.

As soon as we arrived, we were issued our weapons and ammo, and we began filling sandbags to place around our tents. Although we were South of Dong Ha and supposedly out of the range of the enemy guns, manglers were always a threat.

We'd been in Quang Tri for about three weeks when the news of our first casualties hit the company street. Our platoon leader, Second Lieutenant Bruce Wilson, and three others had been picked to recover the body of Lieutenant Donald Matocha, who had been killed on an earlier recon patrol with another company. His body was believed to be in the area of Dong Kio, a small knoll about 1000 meters from the Cam Lo River. The four-man team headed in that direction, and as soon as they approached the hill, all hell broke loose. Gary Meyers and Carlos Dominguez were killed outright; Lieutenant Wilson and radioman Clark Christie lay wounded. Christie called over the airways, pleading for help.

A ten-man volunteer reactionary team from Charlie Company flew into the fray and immediately found themselves in a thunderous fight. Their location had been recorded, and the manglers and rockets flew in with deadly accuracy. The team took out one enemy bunker with the accurate placement of a round from a LAW. Outnumbered, the recon Marines held their ground. Fighting to gather the dead and protect the wounded, they waited for the extraction choppers to rescue them. Overhead the blades of the Huey gun ships beat the air while their guns pounded the enemy below. Suddenly a Ch-46 helicopter dropped into the kill zone.

The pilot flying that day was Major David Altoff, a man who became a living legend by piloting his chopper into the blood dance with steady hands and nerves of steel. With manglers hitting within feet of his war bird, the major waited until all the Marines were on board before he lifted out of the hot zone. Once airborne, he learned that two Marines were missing, so he dropped his bird low, searching for the missing men. When he finally located them on the north side of the ridge, he couldn't find a place to set down. Still under heavy fire, he maneuvered the craft to within feet of the hillside, and the two Marines were able to scamper aboard through the left side door. Another brave soul from the reaction force threw his body over the severely wounded Christie to protect him as incoming mortars pounded them.

Unlike Jesus Christ, Major Altoff couldn't offer eternal life, but he could offer escape from death. When he made this offer, he had no idea if it would cost him his life and the lives of his crew, yet under extreme fire he made it anyway. Five days later he did it again. And again it was men from our company who found themselves in a deadly fight.

"Sky Merchant" from Echo Company had been out for three days. On day three they exchanged fire with two Charlies who were probing them from the rear. When Sky Merchant opened up, the two suddenly had more friends. The fire that hit the team was so severe that it left only Lance Corporal Mark Kosterman unwounded. Once again Major Altoff hovered over a hillside with only the rear wheels of the aircraft touching the earth. Holding steady as the incoming fire increased, he kept his chopper on the ground for ten minutes while mangler rounds hit within feet of the chopper. Ten long minutes while Mark Kosterman and the door gunners ran back and forth under fire to retrieve the dead and wounded. Ten horrendous minutes while gun ships flew overhead trying to stop the incoming.

One Marine from the team sustained a direct hit from the manglers. His body parts were so scattered that they couldn't be retrieved. If it hadn't been for the raw nerve and dedication to duty of Major Altoff, his gun crew, and Mark Kosterman, there would have been even more dead Marines that day. Ernie's good friend, radioman Gary Thomas, was killed on this bloody mission.

The news of our first dead rocked some of the Marines who hadn't yet seen action. It was a sobering reminder that we couldn't take NVA soldiers lightly. They were dedicated warriors who didn't like recon poking around their turf. And although I didn't know it at the time, the NVA had specially trained recon-killer teams whose mission was to hunt down our teams and destroy them. I suppose that could be considered a compliment.

The enemy was cutting up Echo Company, the tension was mounting, and our men were spoiling for a chance to fight back. I can't remember why, but I missed my team's first patrol. It may have been a head cold. A pattern had developed: Every time I flew out of or into Nam, I would catch a cold. Nobody with a head cold was allowed in the bush. A cough could kill the whole team. I was disappointed, but I didn't miss out on any action on that patrol, and it wasn't long before we were summoned to the next briefing. This time I was on the roster.

We double-checked our gear and went to the briefing tent. We were going to an area east of Quang Tri where there had been eight recent contacts between recon teams and larger units of the NVA. We were told that the vegetation in the area was short and sparse—not good news. Without good cover, we would have to move very carefully. At the end of the briefing, the officer in charge casually mentioned that it would be nice if we snagged a prisoner or two. We all smiled at the prospect and hoped we could oblige him.

Our insertion was scheduled for the next morning. The plan was to bail off some trucks as we moved down route 9, allowing us to conceal our deployment and enter the RZ undetected. In war, plans seldom work as discussed, but at least we had a plan, and that was much better than simply following the Marine in front of me with no idea where we were or where we were going.

Due to the open terrain, we took the M-60 machine gun along. Normally we'd leave the heavy beast behind, but on this mission it made good sense to have some extra firepower. If we got caught with no place to run, we could sling some serious fire. There are few things more fearsome than a heavy, barking machine gun.

Tut had a saying: "He who fights and runs away lives to fight another day." That was the way Charlie fought, and this might be the mission where we tested that theory for ourselves. It made sense to me that it would be better to be alive for the next round of killing than to be all hacked up and seriously dead. Dead men don't win wars. The basic concept of warfare is that your adversary wants you dead and you want to return the favor. The rest of it is the "Art and Science" of war. On this mission, we'd be dealing with the basics.

Before sunup we were painting our faces and checking our gear. There wasn't much discussion as we made our last-minute preparations. I saw no apprehension on anyone's face, maybe because the streaks of camouflage paint helped cover any signs of it. I remember feeling slight crosscurrents of anxiety and excitement, but other than that, no strong emotions. My plan was to put one foot in front of the other, go into the jungle, and hope I would come out in one piece.

Yea, though I walk through the valley of the shadow of death, I will fear no evil ... for Ernie, Tut, and these other ugly Marines were with me. Each man depended on the man next to him. If we walked into the dragon's mouth, we would rely on each other to pry its teeth away from our flesh. If today were a bad day, I knew that I would be with men who would not leave me alone in the fire. I felt confident I could do the same for them. Besides, I knew that the NVA had already heard about Meatball and Fudd.

Among our little group was a Navy corpsman who accompanied our team on many missions. I wish I could remember his name, but time has erased it. I kidded him once about his luck of going into the Navy and then ending up following us groundbound grunts around. He smiled and said it was okay. He was doing what he wanted. I admired his attitude and respected his ability to carry all the war gear plus his bulky medical bag. It was good to have a weapon packing "doc" along in case we needed his services. Someday he could save our lives by treating our wounds. If he wasn't needed for medical services, he could fight with us, thereby causing the other side to need his expertise. It was another paradox of war. Take an oath to help stop the bleeding, and if required, make sure the other side will need your services once the shooting stops.

Just like in the movies, the nine of us bailed off the moving trucks. If Charlie was watching our small convoy, we hoped we had him hoodwinked. The hunt was on, but it was yet to be determined who was the cat and who was the mouse.

The vegetation was as advertised. We had to keep moving and hope that we were invisible. If Charlie saw us, maybe we'd look like creeping trees—creeping trees with guns and grenades, painted faces, and funny looking hats. If we got caught in this open range, it would mean a miniature Custer's last stand and another disaster for Echo Company. We didn't need another disaster; we needed to cause one. We needed to show Uncle Ho that we, too, could wreak havoc and destruction. Echo Company really needed to slug back.

Like a short snake, we wove our way through and around the terrain. We avoided trails and picked our way around obstacles. Using a trail was asking for big trouble. Hunters using the game trail could instantly become the hunted. Charlie was an expert at ambush, and we had no business walking on a trail where an impromptu strike could shred us. Take the hard way and work your way around the obstacles. Sweat is always cheaper than blood.

The sweat started to run our paint, and I had to wipe my eyes several times. The salt stung. Mac was smart—he'd wrapped a green bandana under his hat—and I made a note to scrounge one for the next mission. Like a cowboy bandana, it would have many uses. If nothing else, a guy could blow his nose with the thing or use it for toilet paper.

I should have known enough to bring a bandana along, because I once was a cowboy. It was peaceful in those days, riding in the mountains above my hometown, smelling the sagebrush after a rain, admiring God's creation, and listening to the soothing sound of squeaky leather. Everything was usually right with the world when leather squeaked. It meant I was still in the saddle and the woods were not full of mean little yellow men.

Mac was in front of me in the column. I had tilted my head slightly to the ground to let the sweat roll to the earth. The strike came without warning and without noise. The little brown son-of-a reptile reached out and hit Mac's boot with swift precision. Mac never felt a thing, but I jumped back, startled by the swift attack out of nowhere. If he'd been a longer snake, his strike would have caught Mac in the flesh. As it was, the highly poisonous viper was not much bigger than a Texas night crawler. He didn't have enough body length to sink his tiny fangs anywhere above the boot leather. Had he penetrated Mac's skin, Mac would probably have died gasping for air. Side-stepping where Mac had just stepped, I watched the little bastard slither off.

Looking up the column, I could see Tut with the M-60 slung over his shoulder. It was good to see the gun bobbing up and down in this bush. I hoped I was the only one who could see it. Each of us carried some ammo for the gun, adding to our load. Still, there was no load heavier than packing the radio plus all the items of war. Ernie packed the thing like a champ. I admired his stamina and strength.

Our bodies strained against their respective loads. The straps on military packs weren't anything like those on a modern pack-frame. I have seen pack mules lie down when they were overloaded and couldn't grunt one more step. The trick for a human grunt was to balance your load between what you needed to sustain your life and what you needed to take someone else's. Depending on how things went in the bush, one grenade or one bullet could be worth all the food or water in the world.

Considering the open country, it was so far, so good. The snake had scared the heck out of me, but I had managed to stifle the scream in my throat. I wasn't as successful with the stuff in my pants, but that discomfort would have to wait until we stopped.

After about an hour of steady humping, we came to a rise in the terrain that afforded a good view of some low ground to our east. Low ground is bad ground, and moving into it would put us at extreme risk. If we stopped here and watched, maybe the risk would be Charlie's. Below us was a well-used, partially camouflaged trail. Sergeant Johnson directed us to place the claymores while he plotted our position and the coordinates of the trail below.

We placed our claymores carefully and doubled-checked that they were pointing in the right direction. There could be nothing worse than placing a claymore with the wrong side pointing at you. The curvature of the mine was a good way to remember if you had it right. If the mine fit up against your tummy, it was right. It would be a stupid way to die to hit the detonator and eat your own lethal lead. We didn't want to blow ourselves into body bags.

Ernie called in our location and the numbers for the trail. Now we would sit and wait. It felt good to sit with our packs off. The sweat on our backs dried rapidly. It was still hot, and the sparse shade was only slightly better than the harsh sun.

About midafternoon our prey became visible. The excited whispers about movement on the trail set off a silent battle for the one pair of binoculars. We could see the men with our naked eyes, but I suppose everyone wanted to see them up close and personal with the binoculars. We were like kids who had to share a favorite toy, counting the seconds until it was finally our turn to use the glasses. Sergeant Johnson pulled rank and took them. He whispered the numbers as they moved below us.

"There are only four," he said. "We'll let them pass and see who else shows up."

Less than an hour later, another small group walked down the trail. They didn't seem to be in any particular hurry, but we were sitting on pins and needles waiting to slam them with artillery. All of us understood that when the big slugs came, Charlie would know that someone was on their turf. The cat-and-mouse game would intensify, making it a bit more difficult for us to remain the cat.

The next group to appear consisted of twelve NVA with packs and arms. As they walked into the preplotted kill zone, we unleashed the big guns. The first Willy-Peter round landed right on target, so we immediately followed it with fire for effect. The high explosive airbursts were murder. The group screamed and jumped. We announced our savage delight with whispered *oohs* and *aahs*, just as if we were watching fireworks on the Fourth of July.

I never would have thought it could be entertaining to watch men scamper and fall under fire. At the time I felt nothing other than that it was payback time. Charlie was getting what he deserved. It was good to see our manglers rip and tear at the men who had ripped and torn so many around me at the Washout. The estrangement from myself was deepening, but I still didn't realize what was happening. On that day all I knew was that it was good to see the enemy caught in the jungle, in the fire, in the blood. It was good to see Charlie have his own fatal terrain.

Just before dark, 28 more NVA with heavy packs and weapons tried to move through our kill zone. Once again our artillery mangled them. The cries of fear and screams of agony echoed up to our little fort, music to our demented ears. We had done our job and applied our trade. Blood had been spilled, and for a change it wasn't ours.

With the last shred of daylight, we watched seven of the enemy run back up the trail with no packs and no weapons. At least 31 lay dead or unable to move. If the running seven were going after help, we could be in for a long night. We may have won in the daylight, but there was no question in my mind who owned the night. We were in Charlie's night, Charlie's jungle, Charlie's dark. The cat could very easily become the mouse. The night orders came. We double-checked our claymores and weapons.

I hadn't mentioned the snake that had struck at Mac, and I hoped we weren't camped on a snake-infested hilltop. I remembered an old western movie where a cowboy lay frozen in his bedroll because a rattler had decided to cuddle with him in the night. When everyone got up in the morning, they couldn't figure out why this guy was lying there unmoving, with open, unblinking eyes. When someone asked him what was going on, the cowhand wouldn't talk. Finally the trail boss decided that there was something amiss under the bedroll.

"Blink once if there is a snake in bed with you," he whispered.

The one blink solved the mystery, and the cowboys went about trying to smoke the serpent out from under the bedroll.

For a ten-year old kid, this was high drama, and I sat on the edge of my seat waiting for the snake to slither out so he could be killed. The snake died and the cowboy lived. In the movies heroes always live.

I'd drawn last watch with Tut, so if I could sleep, I could get several hours in before it was my official turn to watch and listen. There was another movie where Davy Crockett slept with one eye open. I don't know how Davy did it. I tried it, but when I closed one eye, the other one slammed shut. I woke up many times and listened. Some minor night noises caused some jumpiness, but we passed through the darkest hours without problems. So far we were safe and undetected.

My watch came, and I sat up with my back to Tut's back. We were about ten feet apart, listening for any bad night sounds. I longed for a cup of hot coffee, but I knew that would happen only in my dreams. It struck me how peaceful and quiet it was. It was almost too peaceful. No one farted or snored. The trees didn't even rustle. It was a beautiful night, with stars covering the sky. It's funny, but I can't remember if I could see the Milky Way. I don't even remember looking for it. I do remember that I seldom looked up into the heavens. Simple innocent pleasures like that seemed to have been lost, but for some reason, I didn't miss them. Maybe I thought that the heaven over this strange land wasn't the same one that was over home. Strange how your mind adapts to the situation you find yourself in. Stranger still how you aren't even aware of it.

That night I didn't even think about home or my girl. I didn't think about war, about death, about life, or about what my family was doing. I was in a funnel, and somehow my head had gotten stuck in the small end. All I did before dawn was listen for any unfriendly sound. All I did was listen and wait.

The blessed daylight came and with it more heat. I looked down at the trail and rubbed my eyes. I yawned an almost bored yawn. It scares me to think back and realize just how casual I felt. My nerves should have been arching across each other. There were the night jitters for sure, but as the daylight came, all was well. I turned around and looked at Tut. Then I let my eyes wander over the rest of the team. They tossed and turned as they reluctantly came out of sleep.

At times it seemed difficult to understand the reality of this whole affair. I mean, here we were sleeping on the ground like homeless men with no other place to go. The rifles and grenades were proof that we were in an armed conflict, yet even with yesterday's killing, we all just kind of lay around as if nothing really deadly had occurred. One would think a body would shiver through the night, waiting for something bad to happen. Without question, the devils were on the loose, but on the surface the entire bunch of us seemed about as relaxed as little old ladies shopping for potatoes. Our real feelings—our human-being feelings—must have been coated with some kind of war paint.

A whisper interrupted my thoughts.

"Let's go down and set up an ambush!"

Tut had come up with a brilliant idea of how to start off the morning. It wasn't "Good morning guys; how did you sleep?" or "Did the bedbugs bite?" It was "Let's go down and set up an ambush!"

The team stayed silent. No one spoke or moved his head in agreement or disagreement.

I wished I could have had a cup of hot coffee before I had to think. But we wouldn't be doing any cooking this morning, so I had to mull over Tut's idea with a congested brain. I didn't think it was a good idea or a bad idea. At that point it was still a nonidea. But as Tut explained his line of reasoning, it made an awful kind of sense. We go down there, deeper into the dragon's den, cut off the head of the dragon, and run for our lives with its head bouncing along behind us. When we get tired of running, the choppers come and get us, and we go back for hot showers and a few days of free time. If we're lucky, we snag a couple of smaller dragons, present them to the king, and become instant heroes. Our armor would shine, and we would be inducted into the knighthood of the dragon slayers, the men who ate fire for breakfast.

Translated, all this meant was we go down there, set up an ambush, kill some gooks, and in the process bring a couple of them in as prisoners of war. We still might have to eat some fire, but that's why we got out of bed this morning.

I must give Sergeant Johnson credit. He explained the very serious downside of Tut's idea. We all knew the facts. The area was crawling with the enemy, and we might get caught by a large force and get wasted. We could very easily end up as prisoners or dead. I don't think Sergeant Johnson was speaking out of fear; he just wanted each one of us to fully understand the risk. Nobody except God Almighty knew how many little mean men were walking around down there.

"Whatever we do," the sergeant said, "we can't stay here much longer."

If we stayed on this hill, Charlie would soon find us. We had to move sooner or later, but there was also danger in moving. Charlie was on the move in sizeable numbers. We could very easily bump into him and get caught in a surprise fight. By setting up an ambush, we would at least have the element of surprise going for us.

The idea made sense, and we did something I would never witness again as long as I was in this outfit: We took a vote. Every man would have a democratic say in his future—something very out of the ordinary for a Marine under any circumstances, but almost unbelievable in the middle of a jungle surrounded by communists. Our little circle cast the vote. Thumbs-up and nods of approval went around. The vote was 100 percent in favor of going in.

We checked our weapons and pulled the claymores in. As we touched up our face paint, I smiled inside. We looked like a group of ladies powdering their faces for the big dance. We replenished our war paint and moved out.

We moved quickly. We had to cover the same open ground that Charlie had the night before. If he was watching, yesterday's success could quickly turn into today's defeat. We walked into last night's kill zone and saw the flies feasting on the pools of blood. There were no bodies, but there were several weapons and packs lying around. We tied a line around the packs and pulled them over. Charlie loved to booby-trap anything that might draw a curious tug or pull. But everything was free of explosives, and we quickly gathered what we could and left the flies to their feast. I didn't care if it snowed or not. The snow would cover what we had done, and I wanted Charlie to see the blood and the feasting flies.

Again the savage delight. The damn savage delight.

We moved up the trail until we found enough cover to set our trap.

The claymores were placed on both ends of our in-line ambush. The mine on the right flank would stop any NVA trying to escape; the one on the left would shred those at the head of the column. We would rake the middle with small arms fire. Sergeant Johnson told us that he would spring the trap with his M-16. Once we heard his fire, we were to open up and spread fire on the trail. If possible, we were to wound some of the enemy so we could take them prisoner.

Tut and the machine gun were at the end of our right flank. He would stop anyone from fleeing back up the trial. Again Arty was preplotted with a ring of fire around us. Ernie called in the coordinates, and we settled down for the wait.

The full heat of the sun beat on us. It would be a very warm wait. I took a position under a short leafy tree, and while the shade was minimal, it did help shield me from some of the heat. After about an hour of lying on my stomach and cooking my back, I decided to imitate a hot dog on a skewer and roll. But when I rolled over on my back, I gasped.

Inches from my nose, a bigheaded snake lay staring at me. He was not coiled; he was just looking at me with his cold, beady eyes. I wanted to scream. I wanted to wet my pants. I lay frozen, not wanting the snake to strike. We'd been told to consider every snake in Nam deadly, and I never questioned that instruction. So there I was in the middle of the dragon's den, pinned down by a snake that could kill me in seconds. I couldn't call out for help. Any noise or movement could blow the ambush, and if we lost the element of surprise, all of us could be full of bullet holes. If I lay there frozen and the enemy showed up, a fierce firefight would go on around me while I lay there nose to nose with this reptile.

The trail boss and the rest of the crew were lying prostrate along the trail, completely unaware of my predicament. I had to make a decision: I had to either whisper for help or slither out from under the snake. I choose to pray that the snake was in a lethargic mood and slither out from under him. Inch by inch, quietly, very quietly, I gained six inches. The forked tongue came at me, and the snake raised its head as if to strike. *Dear Mr. & Mrs. Standiford: We regret to inform you that your son....* I don't care what Sitting Bull said—it was still not a good day to die, especially from snakebite.

Finally the snake turned his head and slithered through the tree branches. Oxygen filled my lungs, and I back-crawled. A twig snapped, and Rudd crept over to see about the noise.

"What was the twig about?" he whispered.

Unable to talk, I pointed to the snake in the tree.

I shuttled my position to the left and then took a snapshot of the long green reptile. I'd been on the stairway to heaven, and I had to have a picture of the creature that could have sent me straight up to the Almighty. Since Adam and Eve, snakes have caused a lot of trouble here on this planet. I wish it had started talking to me. I could have gone straight out of Nam under a section eight.

About an hour later, movement on the trail turned the episode with the snake into a memory for later nightmares.

"Four are coming" came the flat-line whisper.

We flipped the selectors on our weapons to full auto and waited for Sergeant Johnson's burst of fire. It was like waiting for the end of time. We were about to start a fight, and if there were more NVA behind this small group, it might turn into a bigger brawl than we could handle.

I could see the legs of the humans walking down the trail. If I'd had extra long arms, I could have reached out and touched them. They walked by in silence, completely unaware of the trap we were about to spring on them. Our silence must end soon. Soon, very soon, the sergeant must pull that trigger. My finger lay on my trigger. Waiting, waiting.... The third human in their line of march walked past my position. Come on, Sergeant Johnson, pull that trigger!

The short burst felled the soldier. The claymores exploded with thunder. Over the sounds of gunfire I heard Tut scream a string of obscenities. The short bursts of the machine gun fire had fallen silent, and Tut was mad. The thing had jammed, and the last NVA was escaping back up the trial. I couldn't see Tut, but he was in hot pursuit of the running enemy, a hand grenade clasped tightly in his hand. Meatball followed him up the trail.

The exploding grenade was the last sound of our attack. Tut came strolling back, smiling that smile.

"The gook's dead," he told Sergeant Johnson. "His arm's up in a tree."

Meatball nodded.

Arty had been called, and now it exploded in its covering ring of shrapnel. Ernie was on the radio talking to the choppers. Two wounded NVA lay on the trail. We took them prisoner at gunpoint, and Doc began to treat their wounds.

The lead man of the group lay in pieces from a claymore blast.

I took a few pictures while we waited for the choppers. So far it had been a textbook ambush. The only thing that had gone wrong was the jamming of the machine gun. If the choppers landed soon, and if there were no Charlies about to swarm down on us, we would soon be airborne back to Quang Tri.

Mac pulled in the claymore wires while we watched the trailhead for movement. Someone had stuck a Marlboro in the mouth of one of the prisoners, and the man inhaled and exhaled very calmly. Doc must have shot him up with morphine. Just seconds before, we had been trying to maim and kill him, and now we were taking care of this wounds. I walked over to take some more pictures, and our eyes met. I will never forget how he looked. His dark eyes looked right into mine. There was no pleading, no sign of fear. Even with his leg and hand wounds, he looked serene and comfortable. Either the morphine had numbed everything to the bone, or this was one brave little man. I will always remember those steady eyes. It struck me that he showed no contempt for us, no hate, just a steady, penetrating gaze. I can still see those eyes as clearly as if I were standing over him today.

The sound of blades hammering the air indicated we would soon be out of here. The CH-46 landed, and we dragged our prisoners inside. Overhead the gun ships provided raking fire for our extraction. If the NVA were coming for us, they were too late.

Rudd and I dragged the Marlboro man into the bird. It was kind of amazing to have an enemy in my grasp after so many months of not even seeing the foe. When our two prisoners and everyone else were aboard, the chopper lifted off. It was about the best feeling in the entire range of emotions. The only thing that could go wrong now was a wayward hit from the ground, and shortly we would be too high for even that.

We landed at "D Med" in Dong Ha. The prisoners were placed on a stretcher and hustled into the tent. We didn't know it at the time, but one of the prisoners had died en route. He had poisoned himself. We all thought he was Chinese because he was almost as big as Ernie was.

As I watched the prisoners being taken into the hospital, I was glad we hadn't mistreated them in any way. I felt no remorse for the ambush, but I still knew myself well enough to know that, had we done something out of line, I would never sleep again. It was still questionable whether I'd been born to kill, but there was no doubt in my mind that I hadn't been born to mutilate.

We boarded the choppers and were transported back to Quang Tri. Captain Raymond met us at the landing zone. We were greeted with broad smiles, proud handshakes, and ice-cold beer. The dragons had been delivered to the king, and we were the heroes of the day. Echo Company had struck back and struck hard.

The debriefing was full of jokes and elation. The teams that were not in the bush turned out to see our spoils. We handed the enemy packs and weapons over to the captain, who beamed when he saw the documents in the packs. It was kind of difficult to hide our emotions. I think we tried to act humble, but we might have come off a little too cocky. As a matter of fact, we had been gutsy, so I suppose we deserved to do a little swaggering. Today's action proved that we would go deep into Charlie's turf and square off with him. It had been a tit-for-tat kind of day, and we had delivered the tat. We had remained the cat.

We hit the showers. It felt good to get the sweat off, but it wasn't purifying as some showers are. I for one felt no remorse for the dried blood on my hands. I was happy to have been a part of thrusting the stinger into the enemy. I didn't even close my eyes as the water turned a faint red and disappeared at my feet.

8
OTHER FACES OF WAR

We were rewarded for our success with a three-day, in-country R&R, and two days after landing with our spoils, we caught a chopper to China Beach.

China Beach was amazing: There was electricity, cold beer, enlisted men's clubs, and activities for almost every taste, including swimming on the beach and baseball games. I didn't know this war could be so comfortable. The only real reminder of it was the constant departure and arrival of fighter jets. Other than that, the place seemed like a dreamworld. Almost everyone wore polished boots and spiffy utilities. I even saw a green beanie in an immaculate uniform with absolutely no sweat under the arms.

Tut, Ernie, and I made fun of the air conditioning and the sanitized folks running around looking important. It was my first exposure to war in the rear, and it confused me. For some reason I had this idea that everyone who came to Vietnam lived much like the brain-dead grunts. Grabbing a can of ice-cold beer or sitting in a lounge chair felt so foreign that it almost made me nervous.

We went to the Post Exchange to shop. Almost anything you could imagine was there. We bought some swimming suits, sun lotion, and sunglasses. We had become tourists, and it felt absolutely strange. We captured a spot on the beach and, of all things, decided to lie in the sun. I would have thought we'd had enough of lying in the sun, but we were a little confused about what to do. I jumped in the surf and went for a short swim. The water was warm and clear. The white sandy beaches were beautiful. A guy could get too comfortable around there and forget there was a war going on.

That evening Doc got a little sideways with too much drink and got into an argument with some big Hawaiian guy. He dropped down into some weird martial art stance and egged the hulk on. To save his life, we took him prisoner.

Our time in paradise was short, and the only thing that went wrong was that they told us to sleep near the airport. Asking a grunt to sleep through the constant sorties of jets landing and taking off isn't the best plan in the world. I thought I could sleep anywhere, but the rumble of the jets kept me awake.

When our time ran out, we hopped a chopper back to Quang Tri. I was almost anxious to get back to what I knew. The R&R was okay, but it seemed more surreal than I could handle. I felt so out of place amid all the spit and polish that it almost wore me out thinking about it. Life seemed much simpler at Quang Tri, where we lived much like campers and our military protocol was very basic. The officers left us alone, and there was no spit and polish.

I don't know if it was sheer coincidence, or if we had spies on the base, but the night after we returned from R&R, we were hit with incoming. It was the first time I could remember manglers at Quang Tri. The interesting part was that most of the rounds landed directly on Echo Company. Was this payback for our ambush? Who knows? But it seemed as if Charlie had located our area and wanted to send a message. Several of our tents were shredded, but all of us made it to the bunkers, and I don't recall any casualties. The manglers did shake things up a bit, but that was normal. I hoped that incoming wasn't going to become a part of my daily existence again. There had been enough at the Washout to last me a lifetime.

Sometime after our R&R at China Beach, I was due for an out-of-country R&R. Sally was in Hawaii—I can't remember why—so I put in for Hawaii for my R&R. Her letters weren't coming as regularly as they once had, and I still felt something was wrong. When a radiophone became available, I got permission to give her a call. My plan was to meet her in Hawaii and get married.

There are good ideas in war and there are bad ideas. I had this gut feeling that I probably wouldn't get out of the war alive. It wasn't an overwhelming premonition; just a nagging suspicion that hung with me. So it was probably a bad idea to get married. But, good or bad, I made the call and told Sally my plans.

Sally said it was a bad idea. As a matter of fact, I don't recall her even saying she wanted to see me. I couldn't believe how distant her voice was. There was no longing on the other end of the phone line. I thought about going to Hawaii to find her and put the matter on the table, but I didn't think I could face the truth. The truth would surely set me free. Even a thick-skinned grunt like me could tell it was over.

A loveless moon had risen, and I wanted to thrust cold steel into its heartless light.

I went down to a bunker to think. There is something about being in the pit of the earth. When I'd received the upper cut of death in that lonely foxhole at the Washout, the earth had seemed to hold me together. The dirt is a good place to mourn; it holds you, but at a distance, without gripping you too hard. It's a place to find yourself and overcome what needs to be overcome. I sat in the dark bunker and let the dirt hold me one more time. No one could see my disappointment, my pain. Once again I had to travel alone. I wished I could get on my knees and pray for guidance, but for some reason I couldn't find God this time either. The dirt had become my most loyal friend.

I suppose my biggest hurt was feeling that no one was loyal anymore. Time after time I'd seen men get slugged by bad mail, but I'd never once thought that I'd lose Sally's love. With the antiwar protests going on and the phrase "make love not war" even showing up Nam, it was like living in some mean little twilight zone. I felt like hammered dog poop. If there had been a pile of dog poop available, and if I'd had a hammer, I certainly would have pounded the crap out of the crap.

I hadn't shed any tears since the day Lieutenant Crary died, and I didn't shed any now. Maybe I should have bawled, so some water from the well could have flushed my soul. I think I wanted that release, but I wouldn't allow it. Tears can show fears. Whatever was going on with my girl, there was absolutely nothing I could do to change it, and in the dirt, in the dark, I made a decision to write her a Dear Jane letter. I would take control of the painful situation and let her know I was done. I could become a stone. Only the rocks live forever because they don't find or lose love, and an island never cries.

I came out of the dark bunker with a plan. I would put in for R&R, and I would not die a virgin. God forgive me, but I would land on some friendly soil, wage war with sin, and let sin win. The serpent had offered me an apple, and I was going to eat of it and become a full-fledged, dirty, good-for-nothing grunt. I figured that if the Almighty sent me straight to hell for it, even hell would be better than this place of gyrating demons.

I put in for the R&R. Stuffing more than a thousand dollars in my pocket, I headed off to Japan, where the liquor went down the hatch and the fast ladies got the cash. In three days I was out of money, in sorrowful shape, and feeling that it would have been better if I hadn't been born.

Before I flew back to Nam, I considered looking into a mirror. Something made me want to find myself again, but I ignored whatever it was. Maybe I was afraid I would see no reflection and realize I'd become a blood-hungry vampire. The dark side controls vampires; they do the bidding of the evil one and cause death and destruction whenever they can. I was caught in a no-man's land—on one side was the light of God, but the dark of the other side held me. Walking away from my spiritual conflict, I found it easier to keep my distance from myself. It was all becoming too confusing; it was too hard to figure, too hard to think.

When I returned to Nam, I kept most of the worldly experiences to myself. Tut and I still argued religion from time to time, but I felt I'd been busted to the rank of private in God's army, and I knew I shouldn't be talking a lot about being holy or righteous.

I had decided to study my enemy in great detail, and I ordered some books on Ho Chi Minh. Tut gave me a sideways look when he saw me reading Ho's book on revolution. I read some of it aloud to him. As I studied, I became convinced that every American in Vietnam should be required to read this man's work. In a speech in 1964, President Johnson had said, "We are not about to send American boys nine or ten thousand miles away from home to do what Asian boys ought to be doing for themselves." I couldn't help but wonder if he and the other politicians who got us into this war had read what Ho said in April of 1965:

> The American people have been duped by the propaganda of their government, which has extorted from them billions of dollars to throw into the crater of war. Thousands of American youths—their sons and brothers—have met a tragic death or have been pitifully wounded on the Vietnamese battlefields thousands of miles from the United States. At present, many mass organizations and individuals in the United States are demanding that their government at once stop this unjust war and withdraw U. S. troops from South Vietnam. Our people are resolved to drive away the U. S. imperialists, our sworn enemy. But we always express our friendship with the progressive American people.

Obviously, Johnson had changed his mind. Just as obviously, the government wasn't willing to do what whatever it took to overthrow the government of North Vietnam. So North Vietnam held on, the war dragged on, and American soldiers who had answered their country's ambivalent call continued to die.

Although it seemed a little odd to study war while at war, I made a commitment to continue my studies between missions. As a part of my I self-education program, I also ordered a Marine Corps mail-order course called "Introduction to Aviation." I figured that if I did get out of there alive, maybe I'd get wings that worked.

The days and missions ran together. We went out many times, but for some reason our team went through a dry spell when we didn't see the enemy. Mission after mission was fruitless. Other teams were making contact, and the casualties seemed to come in waves. We didn't know it at the time, but the rear-end warriors didn't believe our reports of heavy enemy movements in the DMZ and along the Laotian border.

In August of 1968, Ernie, Tut, Mac, Meatball, and I were starting to get short. One day we had a discussion about our short-timer status, and some brilliant scholar in the group concluded that we should all extend our tours. I don't remember which of this group of deep thinkers came up with the idea, but he put it to us something like this: "All of us have close to two years left in the Corps. Do you think they'll send us back for another thirteen months?"

Somebody wondered out loud if any of us could bear up as stateside Marines. Here in Vietnam we were allowed to do our jobs, and nobody messed with us on our free time between missions. All of us understood that it would be quite testing to go back, keep our boots shined, and play war games. We simply couldn't see ourselves as Marines without grenades, ammo, and sweat hanging on us.

Without an official vote, we made the decision as a group to extend our tours for six months. This meant we would get a "free thirty-day leave" and could go home, or anywhere we wanted, for a month. I didn't write home with the news. I figured I'd better tell Mom face-to-face so I'd be there to catch her if she went for the kitchen floor.

I suppose it was at this point in my tour that, without knowing it, I had truly become a warrior. Here was another chance to get while the getting was good, but I found myself willing, even compelled, to stay. With just weeks left before the end of my tour, I had a choice of going home and leaving all this behind or staying with Marines I had come to know and respect. When it came right down to it, I thought only of staying with Tut, Mac, Meatball, and Ernie.

One day Tut asked me if I wanted to go to Saudi Arabia after we got out of the Marines. "They're looking for mercenaries and guys to guard pipelines," he said.

"Well, the money sounds really good," I said.

The job opportunity sounded interesting, but I didn't think I wanted to end up in another hot, sticky country. And though I still didn't know what I wanted to be when I finally grew up, I was pretty sure by now that I didn't want to live by the sword. Maybe someday I should take an aptitude test and discover where my abilities and weaknesses lay. I wondered if there was a good aptitude test for this warrior business. The thought made me chuckle inside. I hedged my reply with a mixture of interest and reservations.

About the same time, word was passed that Third Recon was looking for guys to send to scuba school. Recon Marines were supposed to be both jump and scuba qualified, and the word was they wanted more qualified divers in Echo Company. I figured that if I got scuba qualified, they might not ask me to go bailing out of aircraft. Water never bothered me, but I doubted that I could jump out of an airplane. I raised my hand again. I was getting quite good at this volunteering—and so far, so good.

Tut was skeptical. He said he'd heard that prescuba was brutal. You run, then you swim, then you run. They wanted to see how many they could wash out. The survivors of prescuba would go to the real scuba school in the Philippines. I might not have raised my hand if I'd heard this first, but now it was a matter of principle. I said I'd do it, so I supposed that now I had to.

Tut's comments weren't far off the mark. We swam, ran, swam, did push-ups, swam, and ran some more. When I thought my legs couldn't stand any more, we were back in the water swimming against the current of the Quang Tri River. If they wanted to see me die, they could have just sent me back to the bush. At least there I would die in mortal combat, not of heart failure. The only thing that kept me going was the thought of getting out of Nam for a spell and seeing a new country. Somehow I managed to stay with the program. Many did not.

The military does things in a funny way, and the Marines are no exception. After all the physical torture, we were told that we had to see a doctor to determine if we were physically fit enough to become divers. My body seemed to be fine. The doctor poked and prodded in places I would rather not discuss. The only problem I ran into was in the test for color blindness. They said I couldn't go to scuba school because I flunked it. I couldn't believe my ears. They had punished my body to see how badly I really wanted to be a diver, and now they tell me that they think I'm unfit. I knew I wasn't color-blind; I could see colors just fine. Right then I was seeing everything in a very bright red.

"I am not color-blind," I said.

"Try again," the doctor said.

Flipping through the dotted charts, I could make out only about half of the hidden patterns.

My heart sank, but I wouldn't give up.

"Is there another test I can take?" I asked.

"Nope."

"Sir, they just ran and swam us for three hard days," I said.

The doctor looked at me with a slight trace of compassion. "Tell you what. You go over to the air wing, and if you pass the pilot's test, I'll sign you off."

I don't know if he thought he was passing the buck or not, but I passed the pilot's test. I could tell them what was a green light and what was a red light—not bad for having just a high school education. I was elated. I had argued with an officer and won. I had pushed the limits of insubordination, and had the doctor been hard-nosed, he could have told me to sit down and shut up, and that would have been the end of it. Fortunately he understood my situation, and two days later I caught a C-130 out of Vietnam to go to scuba school.

Although the C-130s were the superbirds of the war effort, they didn't provide any passenger comfort. One daft Marine wanted to know about the in-flight movie and even asked when the stewardess was going to serve drinks. Of course there were no aisles and no trays, and if some poor round-eyed lady had shown up in the middle of this smelly bunch, she would have been mauled. A firefight probably would have broken out just for the right to talk to her.

Typically there were no seats in the cargo bay, and if there were lots of passengers, you were stacked on the floor much like sacks of potatoes. You also had to be careful with your rifle. It was easy to get the barrel too close to a fellow passenger, which made it hard to make good flying friends, especially if the person feeling the cold steel was jungle jumpy. Most of the grunts couldn't have cared less about the inconveniences. They were elated to be getting out of Nam for a richly deserved R&R.

Subic Bay was a stark change from Quang Tri. Military personnel moved about in spit-shined shoes and clean, pressed uniforms. Navy battleships lay almost motionless in the harbor. The spotless New Jersey, with its monster guns, looked almost as if it were in a museum. The happy-go-lucky attitude of Marines and sailors and the absence of choppers buzzing the sky was a radical change from the atmosphere of Nam.

We had 48 hours before we had to report for our first session, and we were told that we could go to the enlisted men's club and get some food and drink. But when we stood at the door in our dull, scruffy boots and our camouflage utilities, we were told that we had to be in khakis or civilian clothes to get in. None of our rag-tag group owned anything but what was on his back.

"You'll have to go to the PX and get some clothes," the bulky sergeant told us.

We asked for directions, and then moved out to find the exchange so we could get outfitted. After a couple of wrong turns and asking for more directions, we found the store and started to enter. Again we were stopped cold at the door.

"You can't come in here dressed like that," a light-in-the-loafers looking sailor said.

So there you have it: another typical military situation. We couldn't get into the EM club without the proper attire, and we couldn't get into the PX to purchase the proper attire because we didn't have the proper attire to purchase the proper attire. This place was a long way from the war, and they acted like it. Rules, rules, rules. We weren't used to all these rules. We'd just come from a place where the rule was the gun, and we owned the guns. Even though some considered us unruly, the bastard sons of the Marine Corps, we showed proper military protocol and stood outside the door in our scruffy boots and dirty bush clothes. Finally a Marine officer appeared, and we explained our dilemma.

"Stand by," he said.

He went inside, and in less time than it usually takes to elect an American president, we were ushered inside the giant store. We hadn't seen this kind of merchandise for a long time. All you had to do was put it in a basket and pay for it, and it was yours. It was like visiting another land. We thanked the officer, who was red in the face for some reason. We wondered if he had gotten himself into some kind of scrape because of us.

"Carry on, Marines," he said as he left the PX.

We bought some spiffy looking clothes and changed into them in a dressing room. Hauling tail to the EM club, we drank stuff I'd never heard of.

In the morning I ate a breakfast that nearly made me sick—in a pleasant sort of way. I hadn't seen real eggs or authentic bacon for over nine months. The hot coffee provided a pleasure that I can't describe with words from this world. Even the toast made me want to compliment to the cook. Ice-cold orange juice went down as if God himself had squeezed the fruit. It can be terrible to consume the things you've done without for so long. I tried not to think about going back to the food and drink in the war zone.

For some reason someone decided we needed another rear-end physical. We'd had one before leaving Nam, and why they thought we needed another was a mystery to me. Maybe they thought our bowels had come loose on the flight from Nam to Subic. Whatever the reason, we were herded onto a ship and given one more exam.

School began at 0500 two days after our arrival. Our day began with running and physical exercise. In the tropics, it's easy to sweat, even at 0500. The sweat reassured me. It had become a way of life; if I didn't sweat, I must be dead. After the run we ate another excellent meal at the Navy chow hall. The food was the best I had eaten since I left home. It was just another reminder on how smart Vern had been.

By 1000 hours we were swimming and getting yelled at by the Navy instructors. Some were former Seals and UDT types. They pretended not to like us Marines, and we pretended not to like them. The problem was that they had all the power, and we had none. To some extent it was like boot camp all over again.

After lunch on the first day we went through a test for claustrophobia. It was an amazing way to find out if a student was afraid of tight, dark places. We were placed in old, hard-hat diving suits. The windows of the suit were painted black. It was like being in a body bag with a helmet and weighted shoes. Obviously I hadn't been in a body bag, but it wasn't difficult to imagine how dark it must be in one of those plastic coffins.

One by one, we were run through some simple maneuvers in a twenty-foot-deep tank of water. Underwater the weight of the suit was minimal. It was just a simple matter of trusting the guy on the surface, a guy who just pretended not to like you. We were told to climb up on a table that was at the bottom of the tank. Then we were told to do a 360 or 180 turn and take three steps forward. These three steps put you off the table and into a short free fall to the bottom of the tank. After about ten minutes of following the voice commands, we were given directions to the ladder. At the bottom of the ladder, we were told to purge the suit and start the climb up.

Purging the suit meant turning off the air valve, so we had to climb the ladder either holding our breath or breathing our own CO_2. By the time we reached the top, we were out of air, and many of us saw tiny little stars just before they opened the window and let in some air. I thought I would pass out. The buggers seemed to know just how long you could go on the residual air in the suit. One man flunked the test. He flipped out when he could no longer hold his breath and the stale air in the suit did not satisfy his natural need for oxygen. It took a couple of instructors to hold him down so they could open the window.

The next test was the pressure test. We were put in a decompression chamber and sent down to 300 feet. The pressure at 33 feet is about the same as one atmosphere. This makes the pressure on the body twice as much as on the surface. The farther down you go, the greater the pressure. At 300 feet we were given a gas mixed with helium to counter the effects of nitrogen under pressure. (The guy who invented Donald Duck's voice must have been a diver on helium.) I failed this test the first time because I couldn't clear my ears. True to form, I'd gotten a head cold on my second day out of Nam, and my stuffed sinus cavities felt as if they were going to blow. I was given two days to kill the cold and try again.

I was very relieved when I passed on the second try. After suffering through prescuba, I wasn't eager to leave the school, and besides, I wanted to stay out of Nam for a spell. The food and drink were at gourmet levels here, and the exercise was a long ways from killing me. I thoroughly enjoyed the new environment, and the thought of getting booted really bothered me. I would have hated to return to my unit and tell them that a blasted head cold had caused me to wash out.

We ran and swam, swam and ran. Our first saltwater dive was in the harbor, which wasn't a pleasant place to be because that's where the ships' sewer systems dumped. Human feces floated by as we entered the water. I hoped that when it was time to surface, I wouldn't come up under one of these piles of floating human waste. The thought of the stuff sticking to my facemask and hair filled me with loathing.

After our swimming test the day before, we'd been paired off. The number one rule of this school was to never be more than an arm's length from your designated partner. My partner, Gary, and I dove to the bottom and swam around, keeping an eye on each other. After they signaled us to surface, I was so busy looking for the floating piles that I didn't see that Gary's mask was missing.

When we broke to the surface, a loud voice boomed at the two of us.

"Where in the hell is your mask!"

I looked over at Gary and saw the problem. We were ordered to return to the bottom and find his mask. I was told not to help, but to go only for safety. We found the mask immediately. We surfaced and nearly collided with a floating pile of you know what.

After we climbed aboard the boat, Gary got a chewing out that made both of us hurt. Losing gear under water was almost as bad as cowardice under fire. Gary promised that it would never, ever, happen again. His eyes looked as if someone had attacked him with battery acid. They were very red and beginning to swell. He tried to ignore the discomfort but soon ran off to the head so he could flush them with fresh water. The salt, human waste, and who knows what else had almost blinded him.

After we showered we had our first classroom session. The instructor seized one more opportunity to belittle Gary about his lost mask. He went on and on about the incident. We had to listen because if we didn't, it was bye-bye, and we'd go back to where we came from.

Every day it was pretty much the same routine. Run, then swim; swim, then run. In the classroom we learned about the science of diving and were tested on the subjects of safety, the behavior of air under pressure, first aid for divers, and all the important book stuff. In the water we were constantly pressed to swim harder and longer. Anyone who said they couldn't go on was cut. As in boot camp, not quitting took a certain mindset. Close your eyes and take the pain. Suck it up and smile as they try to wound your body and kill your soul. Never say die, even if you think you might already be dead.

There was only one incident that could have caused my demise. Seven of us had gone to Clark Air Force Base to get paid. We'd been having too much fun and had spent everything in our wallets. Not wanting to wait for the bus to haul us back to Subic, we decided to hire a Jeepie. This proved to be a nearly fatal mistake. Not long after we left the base, I noticed three other Jeepies following us, each with seven to ten Filipinos inside. Once we were out of sight of the base, our Jeepie pulled over. I knew we were in trouble.

At least twenty thugs immediately surrounded us. The seven of us had formed a tight circle and were ready for combat. One of the bandits spoke good English and demanded all our money. I suppose I was the mouthiest of the group, and I got into a heated argument with him. I was clutching a bottle of rum in a sack. It was the only weapon we had. The little thief got in my face. and the bottle came across his head. One of my buddies blocked a knife headed for my ribs. Fighting, we breached their wall and ran for the jungle.

We found a trail going we knew not where, and after gaining some distance from our pursuers, we slowed to a steady jog. All of us were in good shape; we could a jog all day if we had to. Without a clue where it would lead us, we stayed on the forest trail, and after about twenty minutes of running, we hit pavement. As good fortune would have it, an Air Force bus came lumbering towards us. Waving the bus down, we got on board with the sweat dripping and relief on our faces. We had escaped with our money and our lives.

The final day arrived much too soon. We would be tested first in the pool. The rules were simple: They would strip us of everything, even our swimming trunks; we would put our gear back on while staying under water and buddy breathing; anyone who surfaced failed.

We swam around and around the pool. First they pulled off my mask, and then my tanks. A solid jerk to both feet removed my fins. Finally I was buck naked and bugging my buddy for air. Then they attacked my buddy. Now both of us were in the raw, kicking and fumbling for air and gear. Sucking on the mouthpiece of his tank or mine, we managed to get all our gear on, including our trunks. It was an underwater free-for-all, but we stayed calm and went with the program. If you got air, the rest was a piece of cake.

Everyone made it through the pool test without surfacing. We got some lunch and then took the open-water test. It was even simpler: Descend to 130 feet, hang around for a while, and then go back up. It was quite dark at that depth, but it was no big deal.

All good things do come to an end, and I felt a little pang. I would miss the peace of this place. I had worked hard, survived the training, and was now a fully qualified Navy diver. The corker of being either scuba or jump qualified was that they gave us $55 per month hazardous duty pay. We already got $55 per month combat pay. I was surprised that they found it necessary to pay us for diving. It didn't seem anywhere near as hazardous as combat, but, as I said, the military moves in strange ways.

There was a graduation party on the eve of our last day in Subic. It was relaxing, and some of the graduates kind of overdid it. Most of the class was headed back to Vietnam. A couple of Marines were having trouble with that, and the booze loosened their tongues. Although he hadn't seen a lot of action, one of them apparently had a strong premonition that he wouldn't see his home again. He'd never mentioned this before, and I found it difficult to sit and listen to his fears. We all knew we could die, but this was the first time any of us had let those thoughts get to us. When the Marine began sobbing, I found an excuse to leave and told his buddy to throw him in the pool. He hit the water cursing and smiling. It appeared the spell of the booze had been broken.

I didn't see the upset Marine again until the next morning. The darn fool was leaning against the showerhead with cold water running down his back. His buddy was also leaning against the wall. The two were naked and almost blue from the cold water. Someone said they'd been in the showers for almost three hours, trying to sober up before our flight back to Nam. From the looks of things, they might have been slightly sober, but they were in danger of hypothermia.

We dragged their cold, wet hides out of the shower and threw blankets over them. We had only two hours to get these guys presentable, and it looked as if it might take a miracle to get them fit to travel. After an hour of piling blankets on them, a miracle did happen. Without a word, the two threw off the blankets off and got dressed. They acted as if nothing had happened, and by the time we hit the airport they looked pretty darned good. There was no more talk about going back to Nam.

I don't know if either one of them made it home or not.

9
OFTEN TERRIFIED, NEVER BORED

I returned to Quang Tri the same way I'd left. The team, still healthy, caught me up on the news.

In my absence a Vietnamese general had shown up and presented our platoon with high praise and a Vietnamese Cross of Gallantry. Apparently the NVA had phoned in to complain that our little band was hard to deal with, and the office warriors were pleased with our performance. Ernie later told me that after the impressive assembly, our platoon was ordered to attend a work party. Fill a sandbag, burn the honey pots, earn a medal. Or was it earn a medal, fill a sandbag, and then burn the honey pots? Sometimes things were out of order.

I think the best part about being in this war was that you never knew what was going to happen next. Between missions there always seemed to be someone to stir things up. If you could imagine it, it was probably going to happen. It was just a matter of who was going to do what and when. Boredom was not a problem. Even if we were lounging in the rear, there always seemed to be something happening.

One day the ammo dump went up in smoke and shook the earth. It was far enough away not to cause concern, and we just sat and watched the billowing smoke as if it were a Saturday afternoon matinee. The smoke looked akin to what we produced when we burned the honey pots, and some lounging Marine said it looked as if Charlie was burning his crappers.

Due to a command decision, Mark Kosterman was no longer allowed to set foot in the bush. He had earned the respect of all of us, and not a soul thought it a bad decision. During my absence, Mark had become the company thief, and one day he "borrowed" a deuce and a half from some Army unit. We needed the truck for some project, and Mark made the hit. After we were finished with the rig, Mark took it to the ammo dump so the Army could at least find it. The truck went up in smoke with the rest of the dump. It could have been the truck's burning tires that caused the black smoke, not the NVA burning its waste.

An Army officer came around asking questions about his demolished truck. Someone had tipped him off that the thing had been in our camp, and he was on a mission to locate the thief. We convinced him that we hadn't seen his truck and that we didn't have any idea who had stolen his beloved green machine. By this time, we were experts at denial, and the Army man left our camp empty-handed and confused.

Mark nearly got shot during a night raid for some plywood. The plan was to sneak into the Seabee compound and confiscate some sheets for another project someone had dreamed up. The plan went well up to the time of the escape, when a Navy chief saw the jeep and trailer pulling out with the load of procured material. He yelled as loud as he could for the jeep to halt, but Mark goosed the throttle and made his get-a-way. The chief fired two 45 rounds into the back of the trailer. The flying lead only added to the color of Mark's story.

Ernie and some other tough guy had gotten into a mock knife fight. That is, the knives were real, but the fight was pretend. Even with no malice intended, Ernie ended up with a deep gash on one of his hands. We weren't allowed to destroy government property (our bodies), and if we couldn't stand duty, we were in trouble. Even sunburn was a big no-no. Not wanting to endure further pain if the C.O. found out about his wound, Ernie patched it the best he could. Unfortunately, the wound turned black and nasty out in the bush, and he had to seek medical treatment from one of the corpsmen. I can't remember what he used to bribe the doc, but the injury remained a well-kept secret.

One night a running battle ensued between two team members in another platoon. Who knows what started things off? Among young, aggressive Marines, it sometimes didn't take much. The two had exchanged words and fists earlier in the day. Whatever the problem was, one of the Leathernecks was not about to let the dispute die a quiet death. When his adversary was sleeping in the team tent, he attacked. His method of attack is not listed anywhere in the manual of fair play. It's been said, however, that all is fair in love and war. Gathering and stacking empty ammo boxes, the attacker elevated himself above his sleeping foe. As water always seeks the lowest level, the urine landed dead center on the sleeping Marine's face. When the wet sleeper awoke, the team tent was pretty well destroyed.

The worse thing I did (that I will tell you about) was raiding the supply tent for some new type of chow that was supposed to be issued soon. They'd told us we were going to get some freeze-dried rations for the bush. They were supposed to be both tasty and light, so another perpetrator and I decided it was time to give them a taste test. We sneaked in, grabbed a couple of cases, and held our own little tasting party. The new food was much better than the old C rations. We never got caught, and the midnight snacks we enjoyed made the theft worth the risk.

There always seemed to be somebody who could come up with something that made the days a little brighter.

On Easter morning in 1968, Ernie stumbled out of his team tent to take care of the normal morning business that concerned Mother Nature. Down the company street there were what were called piss tubes, which allowed liquid body waste to flow underground. Ernie was standing there half-awake doing his natural business when three Marines in spiffy three-piece suits strolled by.

Fearing that he had lost his mind or was experiencing some weird daydream, Ernie did a double take. Quickly finishing his chore, he spun around to make sure his eyes were seeing right. Sure enough, three guys were walking leisurely down the street as if the suits were the uniform of the day. Many of the Marines who went on R&R purchased expensive three-piece suits at a fraction of their stateside prices. Wearing one of them could make a grunt feel like a tycoon, and that day three Marine moguls were on their way to Easter Mass.

Ernie hustled back to his tent, waking up Marines as he made his way up the street. Heads poked out of tents to watch the three saunter by. It was an amazing sight to see. With an air of aloofness, they held their heads high. No one spoke, but we all smiled at the threesome walking down the dirt street in high fashion. Against the green background of tents and the half-naked reconners peering out at them, they definitely shone.

I happened to notice their feet. Their grungy jungle boots didn't quite match their dress, but from the feet up, their fashion statement was excellent. The only thing that could have improved the scene would have been if a round-eyed girl in a pretty Easter dress had been tucked under the arm of each one of them.

Only in our dreams.

The three classical gassers had provided a moment of comic relief, something that was always welcome and never forgotten. The funny part about the whole thing was that they never cracked a smile. Either they were excellent stand-up comics, or they were in a reverent mood as they made their way to worship. Whatever the case, we talked about them most of the morning. I think I missed church myself because we sat around smiling too long. God bless 'em, whoever they were.

We had been inserted by chopper and were again scouring for Charlie. On the second night we set up the normal harbor site, protected by claymores and the standard restless night watches. It wasn't my watch, but I was kind of up and down most of the night. At about 0300 I was almost drifting off again when I heard some moaning about three positions over from my "bed." The noise concerned me. It sounded as if somebody was either having a good time in his dreams or was in actual pain. Usually in the jungle it's pain before pleasure, so I belly-crawled over to the moan.

It was Tut. "Something's in my pecker," he whispered.

"I'll get a poncho and a flashlight," I whispered back.

Belly-crawling around to get the needed items, I undid my poncho and woke Sergeant Johnson for the light. Quietly I threw the poncho over Tut's head and mine. We didn't want to let our little light shine. A shining light can be seen a million miles in the dark and bring instant disaster.

With our cover secure, Tut unbuttoned his pants.

There we were, the agnostic and the believer face-to-face under a hot, stuffy poncho.

"See what's in there," Tut said.

I hesitated. I really didn't want to investigate the problem.

Tut hit me in the arm. It was obvious he was in misery.

I took a look. It wasn't a picture easily painted with words, as I've never attempted to describe a dark little bug with its body more than halfway down a man's urethra canal.

Leaning up from his enormous (Tut's version), hard-to-see (my version) manhood, I gave him the bad news.

"Looks like some kind of tick."

"Pull it out," Tut pleaded.

I thought for a microsecond and replied, "I'll hold the light."

"No, I'll hold the light."

"No, I'll hold the light."

"Tut, *I will hold the light!*"

It's hard to argue when you whisper. It's even harder when you're face-to-face under a hot, stuffy poncho. Because it wasn't my tick, I held on firmly to the flashlight. I knew that if Tut captured the light, I'd have to try to pull out the little bug. I would've been more comfortable dressing a sucking chest wound than becoming an apprentice penis machinist.

Tut pulled on the mean little bug and then heaved a sigh of relief. I think the last pull hurt like a son-of-a-gun, but he endured the pain as quietly as possible. He only let out a soft moan, yet I cringed. Any noise at night was like a cannon going off in church.

Before I went to sleep, I rummaged in the dark for a battle dressing and placed it in the proper position to protect myself from the kind of attack Tut had just endured. It was the only time I ever I wished I had on underwear. The skivvies would have helped hold the protective dressing in place.

It was a good thing that Tut was tough enough to remove the tick. It would have been quite awkward to call for an emergency extraction. I could hear the radio transmissions in my head. Poor Tut would never have lived it down.

Bury Me With Soldiers

One day we came in off yet another mission. The patrol had been difficult, not because of Charlie, but because of the topography and the elements. The terrain had been steep and the weather hot, and we had trouble keeping enough fluid in our bodies. Locating water had been our biggest challenge, and during much of the mission we were forced to hold up in an effort to conserve our resources.

On about the third day I was lying in the shade craving a hamburger and a giant cup of ice-cold Pepsi. The cup kept dancing in my mind, as if some unseen force were taunting me with this vision of all the liquid I could drink. We've all seen movies where some guy dying of thirst in the desert suddenly goes crazy when he sees a mirage of an oasis. The sun must have been cooking my brain, because my personal mirage was this blasted ice-filled cup of cola, and it was about to win its war for my sanity. Every time the cup swung by in my brain, my throat got dryer. I had the strangest urge to jump up in the jungle and scream, and then guzzle cola.

We were peacefully extracted, and all of us guzzled as much water as we could hold before the debriefing. Afterward I hit the showers. Some Marine was already soaking up the shower when I entered. A familiar noise came from his stall, and apparently he was quite proud of it.

Because I had eaten C ration beans in the bush for breakfast, I was as heavily armed as he was. I fired a volley back at the ill-mannered joker.

"Peace brother," he said, laughing.

It probably wouldn't have hurt if Emily Post had found her way into our uncouth band. Using us for study material, she could have written a manual on the proper etiquette for grunts. She could have called it *Etiquette Whilst Grunting* or *Grunting With Style and Good Manners*.

Things were beginning to change, and not all of the changes were for the better. Our original team was being split up. Rudd and Green rotated out, and then Sergeant Johnson. Mac went with me, Meatball took on a batch of his own, and Ernie and Tut stayed together. Mac, Ernie, Tut, Meatball, and I would all go home on thirty-day leave as our times came up. In the meantime we continued our missions and kept looking for and mixing it up with Charlie.

One night after our team's breakup, Tut and his team were out near the Cua Viet River. In the dark, Charlie showed up unannounced right in the middle of Tut's night harbor. Charlie didn't know that Tut and his team were there, and Tut didn't know that Charlie was out on a night hike. When the two met, all hell broke loose. Tut decided to make them think they had run into a major force instead of a seven-man band of wily teens.

Tut took his men right up the middle of the good-sized enemy force. He figured that if they thought they had disturbed a large hornet's nest, they would take flight. The bold plan worked. Charlie ran for his life up the trail with Tut and his men on his tail. Tut's brave, crazy night charge routed the enemy in confusion and blood.

I don't remember the number of enemy killed that night, and it doesn't matter. When one of Tut's men told me the story, I shook my head and laughed. It was what I would expect from him. This country was lucky he was on our side and not Charlie's. The judge had made a wise decision not to put Tut in the slammer.

After yet another mission, Ernie told me that after the team had carefully set up their night harbor, he had heard something in the dark that disturbed him.

"Do you hear that music?" he asked Tut.

Tut strained to hear, and finally he heard it too.

While they were sitting in the dark trying to figure out where the music was coming from, a trap door suddenly sprang open. A Charlie climbed out of the earth and took a leak. The team had camped right on top of an underground complex. The team waited in suspense for the mole to go back in his hole. Finally, after long, tense minutes, Charlie walked back to the trap door and disappeared into the earth. Deciding that this campground was a little too congested, Tut picked up the team, tiptoed out, and found another place to camp.

Tut was amazing. In one of our discussions I bluntly asked him if he ever worried about getting wasted.

"Nah," he said, "I've had my fun."

I believed him. Tut was so cool, so composed under fire that it almost scared me. He was constantly looking for a fight, and he handled his men so well that he never had anyone wounded or killed. He wore this cocky smile in the bush; he had confidence in himself and it showed. When I was in the bush with him, I had complete confidence that no matter what happened, he would be right next to me slugging it out. I knew if Charlie pinned me down and bloodied me, Tut would be there.

I also knew that if I ever got a tick, Tut would hold the light.

There was one incident after another with Tut and his team, and I can't recall all of them. Maybe the best way for you to get an idea of his fighting ability is to take a look at some of his citations in the appendix. He was also awarded the Navy Commendation Medal for his services and bold fighting spirit. These awards were richly deserved. As I have already said, there was no better man to fight with, even if the ticks did almost get him.

For his part, Ernie earned the reputation of being one of the calmest and most dependable radioman in the battalion. The one person who always had to remain calm was the radioman. If he stuttered or clammed up under fire, things could rapidly go from bad to worse. A self-composed radioman was just as important as bullets, grenades, and choppers. For his devotion to duty and professional service, Ernie was awarded the Navy Commendation Medal. The text of his citation is in the appendix.

Ernie had gone home for his thirty-day leave. The interesting thing about guys coming and going was that when they left, it was like they had never been with us. Even though we were friends, when Ernie left I felt as though he was just another Marine who had gone home. I carried on, not thinking much about his absence. The bonds of this war experience were strange.

After about forty days, Ernie still hadn't made it back to us. I didn't even realize he was overdue until an office warrior made a comment about him being AWOL. It wasn't like Ernie to do something different than what he said he was going to do, and I found it hard to believe that the big beluga wasn't going to come back. It took a while to sort out what had happened, but it finally became clear that Ernie was lounging in Okinawa with a broken leg.

There are many things you do not want to do to a Marine. The top three on this list are (1) make fun of his mother, (2) ask him to reenlist, and (3) get between him and his food. Some fool had broken rule number three and had tried to cut in front of Ernie in the chow line at Oki. Ernie was not about to let this rule be ignored. A fight broke out, and Ernie and the rule breaker tumbled body over body down some concrete stairs. In the tumble, the weight of his adversary broke Ernie's leg.

"I moaned in pain," Ernie told me later, "and the guy rolled me over to see if I was all right. It was the strangest thing. He patted me on the arm and then picked me up and threw me over his shoulder and packed me to sick bay."

There were no hard feelings, and the guy came in and checked on Ernie a couple of times after the docs set his leg.

Intelligence and communications aren't two of the military's greatest strengths, and the report of Ernie's condition took its sweet time making it to Echo Company. As a matter of fact, when Ernie arrived, the office warrior had just sent a letter to Ernie's parents stating that he was AWOL, and he had to rummage through tons of mail to retrieve the letter.

I don't remember how many weeks Ernie lounged around being waited on hand and foot by pretty round-eyed nurses and grumpy corpsmen, but finally one day he limped into the tent. We greeted each other as if he had just come in from a mission.

Meatball always had ways of entertaining us when we were in the bush. Once when we had just finished scouring our RZ and come up empty-handed, we holed up on some high ground to wait for our extraction. Meatball had run out of smokes and had bummed all he could from the rest of the team. On this hill he found some tubular grass. We watched and asked no questions as he busily gathered and dried it.

As usual, the heat dried things rapidly. Meatball dug in his pocket for some matches, lay back in the shade, and lit the grass. Inhaling, he closed his eyes and let out a sigh of pleasure. The smoke came out with the sigh. We watched intently to see if it was as good as he was letting on. He almost fooled us. Then suddenly he gagged. He had to bury his face in the dirt to cover the noise. If we'd been in the position to laugh out loud, it would have been a total uproar. I held my sides and put my hand over my mouth.

Laughing in silence really hurts. I was laughing so hard that I thought I was going to explode. It almost became more important to let it out. I was about to die, and it would be hard to determine the cause of death.

Then there was the time Meatball decided to eat a snake. I don't think he was out of chow; he just wanted to eat the thing. We watched him skin it and took side bets on whether or not he would actually consume the reptile. Using a heat tab for fire, he cut small chunks and roasted the meat over the miniature campfire. He ate about half the thing and then took a snooze. After a while he woke up and belched. He had a terrible stomachache. He got sicker and noisier. Compassionately, we didn't make any smart remarks about his culinary experiment.

On another mission when Meatball was walking point, he was caught in a frontal assault by some fast-charging pigs. The creatures startled him so much that he shot the point pig and then stood shaking in his tracks. The rest of the team thought he'd made contact with Charlie, and we hit the dirt. After a frightful pause, Meatball broke the silence.

"Anyone want pork for dinner?"

The thunderclap of the shotgun had ruined our appetites. We called for an extraction because of the noise we had just made, but we were told to carry on. Rear-end warriors had no idea what it was like to break the silence of the jungle and tell the whole world we were here. It strung the nerves tight and rattled the mind. We had instantly become the mice, and we looked for a good place to hide from the cat.

Bury Me With Soldiers

In the quest to get as many reconners scuba and jump qualified as possible, the word was passed that anyone wanting to go to jump school should raise his hand. My fear of heights hadn't diminished, so it didn't make a lot of sense for me to go around jumping out of choppers or airplanes. Besides, it was heart thumping enough to get inserted by chopper. It would mean double duty for my cardiac system if I were floating above the jungle floor with a large silk sign above my head. In my opinion, a parachute was a set of wings that didn't work. Wings go up and down. Parachutes only go down, usually into places where it would undoubtedly be better to be going up.

The upside of the whole deal was that those silver wings looked pretty cool on a macho Marine's chest. I told the gunny I would think about it and get back to him in the morning. Tut overheard my discussion and said something to the effect of "Why don't you just strap a 2 x 4 on your arm so your hand will always be up when they ask for volunteers?"

I decided that if they gagged and blindfolded me, I could indeed jump out of an aircraft. I raised my hand again. The jump school was scheduled for the following week. I became quite jingled up inside. I wanted those wings, but I wasn't sure that I could force my body to step out into very thin air. I never got to find out. The school was canceled two days before I was to leave. I would never be a "fearless man who jumps and dies," and those silver wings would never end up on my chest. But I wouldn't die of a heart attack during a free fall either.

I still wanted to fly, though. Over time my love of the helicopter had only increased, and I put in for an interservice transfer. My crazy plan was to get transferred into the Army and wrangle my way into warrant officer school and beg and plead for chopper pilot school. When I handed my papers to the commanding cfficer, he looked at me with a hint of contempt. I don't think he understood my motives.

"You know if this goes through and you end up flying for the Army, you'll be right back here," the captain said in a very serious tone.

"Yes, sir. I figured that's what would happen," I said. "But it would be worth it to fly one of those birds."

I don't know if the captain filed the request or not. I never heard from the Army, and the captain never said another word about it. I don't know if he thought I was being a traitor, but I knew it would be impossible to fly for the Marines without a college education. I'll always wonder if the captain used my paperwork for toilet paper.

One ritual that caught on was for a Marine who had just returned from a thirty-day leave in the States to flip up his shirt to show off the growth caused by good cooking and cold beer. One joker even measured and recorded the swollen bellies. We were easily entertained, and looking at some well-fed Marine's stomach was almost as good as watching a first-run movie. Well, almost.

In mid-November 1968 I took my 30-day leave and went home. As luck would have it, I had to leave home just a week before Christmas. It was probably just as well, but it wasn't easy to leave the family when joy to the world had been so misplaced.

In my travels back and forth, I removed my Marine uniform and went under cover as a civilian. I'd heard stories of people spitting on American servicemen, and I was in no mood to land in a situation like that. To be honest, I wasn't sure I could keep my cool if someone hassled me. I didn't know if I would walk away, or if I would get myself in some serious trouble. When you're not sure how you'll handle a conflict, it's probably better to avoid trouble altogether. All I wanted to do was get home and get back without any hassles from anyone.

I landed at L.A. International, and as I stood at the ticket counter, I smelled putrid smoke. Turning around to find the source of the smell, I saw a hippie-looking dude standing there with small flames crawling up his dirty sheepskin vest. As the flames began to grow, the fool tried to set the other side of his vest on fire with a lighter. His eyes looked like they had been transplanted from a cobra. They were glazed and the pupils were missing. I turned back to the counter thinking, *Burn, baby, burn.*

Over the years I have scolded myself for my cold, uncaring attitude, but the guy pissed me off. At the time I felt he deserved to burn for being stupid enough to set himself on fire. In the place I had just left, it was a struggle just to stay healthy, and here this drugged-out piece of dog meat was trying to burn himself up. In my war brain, I figured he was just another draft dodger who had stayed home to fry his brain while we fried in the sun.

As the "flower child" was escorted out of the lobby, I ignored the commotion behind me and paid for my ticket. The ticket lady shook her head at me. I didn't know if she thought I was a big butt for ignoring the fool, or if she was shaking her head at the smoking dummy. I really didn't care.

I left the ticket counter and headed for the restroom. When I entered it, there were two men having sick sex. If this was the "City of Angels," I was ready to catch the first jet plane back to hell. I actually considered doing just that. I'd been on American soil less than thirty minutes, and I had felt a whole lot more comfortable in Vietnam than I was feeling in this human septic tank. Fortunately, I knew that things at home wouldn't be anything like they were in L.A.

The thirty days at home seemed like only twenty-four hours. Before I knew it, I was on my way back to Vietnam and the life I had come to know. Mom's cooking had put some extra pounds on my gut, but I knew it wouldn't take long for the heat to melt the fat away. Come to think of it, I never saw a fat Vietnamese. I know that when the heat hit, most of us ate only one meal a day.

It was strange, but I almost felt more at home in Vietnam than I did back in the States. I didn't understand my own mixed bag of buried feelings about life, death, and serving my country, much less the turmoil at home. The country was tearing itself apart at home while we were tearing the hell out of things in Vietnam. The problems at home weren't the biggest morale boosters. In Vietnam I had come to know those around me, and there I felt a strong spirit of companionship that was missing in the States. It was really a mixed-up mess of fuzzy thoughts.

I was ready to get back, yet I found myself in a lousy mood when I hit Quang Tri just two days before Christmas. It might have been better if I hadn't gone home. In 13 months in this raspy land, I'd almost forgotten about the comforts of home. Now I'd been reminded, and I think I really wanted to be home for Christmas.

I had no one to blame but myself. I could have been home for good by now, but some damn fool had thought it wise to extend, and I had agreed. I also kicked myself for not requesting a rear area job. I could have put in for supply, the armory, or even company thief. Instead, I thought I should stay in the bush. Sometimes I wondered if I'd been born with part of my brain missing.

Mom had asked me why I was going back. I had no reason she could understand. How do you communicate something you really don't understand yourself? I still thought the war was a just cause, but more than that, I think I was growing to like the excitement of the bush. However, I could also tell that my anxiety level was climbing every time I sat on the LZ waiting for the choppers to insert us. I had these mixed feelings of being invincible and mortal. Maybe I loved the excitement, but I hated the mortality of those who were getting wasted. Maybe I was simply going back to kill more gooks and didn't want to admit that to anyone, including myself. Whatever the reasons, I had said I would, and here I was.

When they asked me to stand line watch, I nearly told them to stick it. Nevertheless, Christmas day found me in a foxhole guarding the lines at Quang Tri. There was a Christmas truce, and most of the teams were standing down for the holiday. I can remember being really pissed. I felt about as jovial as Scrooge.

To make matters worse, Mac was my foxhole partner. Now, as I have said, Mac could get pretty cranky, and he didn't like standing watch on Christmas any better than I did. We were a pair to draw to for this watch. For any Charlies even thinking about testing our lines, this would be an excellent day to die. Merry Christmas! Bah! Humbug!

Into this festive atmosphere there suddenly walked a short, chunky girl from the American Red Cross. "Would you like to but a donut?" she asked.

I couldn't believe my ears. *Would we like to buy a donut!* What kind of fool had the audacity to think we would buy donuts on Christmas day and then send a girl out on the wire to peddle them? She had no weapon, no grenades. She wasn't even wearing jungle boots. What was this war coming to?

We let the poor girl know that if she wanted to peddle donuts, she was in the wrong neighborhood. She left in tears, and we laughed at her and her donuts. Whoever you were, I apologize for being rude. It just wasn't a good day to try to sell me a donut. Besides, I never had a wallet on me in a foxhole, and I thought it very naïve that someone thought I did. To top the whole thing off, I wondered why they asked us to *buy* a donut. Couldn't the Red Cross afford to donate them to two grungy knights of freedom?

I was glad when Christmas was over and done. I can't remember ever being in a fouler mood than I was on that day, and I was glad to get things back to normal.

By early 1969, however, things were anything but normal in Vietnam. After the assassination of Martin Luther King in 1968, racial tension had begun to manifest itself in small ways. It was never said in the open, but I believe most African-Americans held every white man in the States, and maybe even in Nam, responsible for Dr. King's death. By 1969, black power was showing up, and race relations were deteriorating fast.

The Marines had begun drafting men to fill the numbers they needed for the war, and we were getting new guys in from stateside who brought new attitudes from home. Some of them complained about all the little things the rest of us had become accustomed to. One little boot was whining about the lousy chow and the absence of beer. I looked at him and told him to go try the real grunts for a while. His smug smile nearly caused my fist to meet his face. This dummy had no idea how good he had it. I wished that every new recon guy could spend some time with the line troops. I hadn't forgotten my roots, and that Marine needed to understand that although we were called "super grunts," we lived like kings compared to the bush hogs.

As time passed, I would wish that our original team had stayed together. I would learn the weighty responsibility of making decisions under duress and find myself worrying about the well-being of the Marines under my command. I would learn that I could never be a general. If I had had to sit and read the daily reports of the American dead, I think I would have snapped. Had I understood all of this at the time, I would never have become a team leader.

A THOUSAND WORDS
all pictures by author

C. Wayne Standiford
AKA Fudd, Elmer Fudd

The Young and the Innocent
Infantry Training Regiment
Camp Pendelton, California

Ambush?
Lima Company 3rd Batallion- 3rd Marines
Near the Washout

A Grunt's life, On the hunt for Charlie.
Lima Company 3rd Batallion 3rd Marines
The DMZ

Out of Choppers and down the rope
Recon training Okinawa

Echo Company sign.
A welcome sight after being extracted from the Bush.

Home Sweet Home
The team tent

Echo Company strikes back.
Sgt. Steve Johnson (kneeling)
Mac pulling in claymore wires
Doc packing his medical bag
after treating the prisoners wound's

With prisoners aboard we are heading home.

Snakes, ticks, leeches, Charlie and man-eating tigers. This 300 pound tiger tried to eat a Recon Marine. A week after this attack a grunt Marine was killed. In 1970 a Marine from 1st Recon was killed by yet another tiger. So many ways to die, hard to stay alive.

Incoming! The well placed rocket landed dead center of this tent.

My last extraction from the bush. The pilot was a little cranky about hanging around for a photo shoot, but smiled when I said, "CHEESE!"

PART III
SOLDIERS ALL

*"It is well that war is so terrible,
or we should grow too fond of it."*

Robert E. Lee

10
SO MANY WAYS TO DIE

There were so many faces, and though the names have been lost to time, I can still see them plain as day. One is the face of a Marine who extended and used his IQ to request a job in the rear for his extra six months. I remember that he had served his team well in the bush and that his peers respected him.

When he came back from leave, he was put in charge of the armory, where we stored shotguns, M-60s, and other special weapons. His job was to keep them ready and keep track of who had what. I chatted with him on several occasions. He was always pleasant and mindful of his duties. One day he fell sick with a high fever, and thinking it was just a common flu virus, the doc sent him to sick bay. The Marine died shortly after falling ill.

Ernie, Tut, and I talked about his death. In our war brains we figured that dying from an illness was an ignoble way to die. All three of us felt that it would be better to die full of holes in a fight than to get sick and die. It was one of the few times we actually discussed a fellow Marine's death, I suppose because the unusual circumstances raised a flag of alarm. In Vietnam it was so hard to stay alive, and there were so many ways to die.

When I'd returned to Quang Tri from scuba training at Subic Bay, I'd met our new company commander, First Lieutenant Carl Myllymaki. This man had a two-word phrase that became one of the most imitated phrases in the company. Whenever he was pleased with something one of us did, he would say, "Outstanding Marine!" Almost daily someone would use this phrase, and it would usually elicit some knee slaps and a smile or two. Lieutenant Myllymaki was an enlisted man's officer. He would talk to us as his equal, and most importantly, he'd leave us alone as long as we didn't cause too much havoc around camp.

The time came when Lieutenant Myllymaki was getting short. I don't remember how many days he had left before he rotated out, but he was short enough to have ignored any impulse to go into the bush. To be honest, I don't know how many missions he had gone out on, but someone told me that the lieutenant wanted to make one last one before heading home. I don't know if it was the first day or the third when his team ran into trouble, and I don't remember if it was a booby trap or a firefight that claimed him. I don't remember much at all about the incident, but I suppose it doesn't matter. Death is death, and it came calling again. Myllymaki sustained severe wounds; choppers flew in to rescue the team and get the wounded out of the bush. The lieutenant's last remarks as he lay dying on the floor of the helicopter were words of apology to his wife.

Black on black. Blood on blood. The damn moon didn't have enough guts to show its face. By now I had learned that war makes no concessions and shows no favoritism. It doesn't care who you are or what you did. Again, if there was an order of death, it seemed out of order.

The silence that descended on the company was laden with sadness and lasted longer than any I can remember. It was a heavy hush. The normal rear-area horseplay was nonexistent. I don't think there was one Marine in Echo Company who hadn't liked and respected our skipper, and it was as if our little tribe of warriors had lost its beloved chief. It wasn't the first blood of Echo Company, and it wouldn't be the last, but in some ways it seemed the most fatal blood to date. There were Marine officers, and there were good Marine officers, but we had lost an Outstanding Marine officer.

No one used that two-word phrase for a spell. Sorrow ran deep, anger deeper, blood lust to the bone. Some announced brave plans for a bloody payback, but tears didn't come out of our wells, because the pumps were still jammed. We picked up the pieces and soldiered on. Call it duty, desire for revenge, or whatever you want; we had no other options. And eventually we began to use the lieutenant's famous phrase again.

When electricity came to Quang Tri via generators, at first I thought it was a great luxury to have, but later I changed my mind. For one thing, it was tempting to become complacent about going into the bush when there were too many comforts in the rear. For another, along with electricity came tape players and music, which began to cause some division among the troops.

The conflicts arose when some of the Brothers would crank up their soul music. Of course someone else would crank up the rock 'n' roll. Most of the time the gunny would yell for everyone to turn down the music, and the matter would be settled. Nevertheless, it was an added source of tension that we didn't need.

Racial tensions had continued to climb, and a few night fights had spilled some blood. I hadn't been around African-Americans much until I joined the Marines, and when black jive and black power hit, it was like being caught in some fascinating crosscurrent. I had no ill feelings towards the blacks. I figured their blood was as red as mine, and if they treated me with respect, I certainly had no problem reciprocating. I admit that I didn't feel any remorse when I learned that Mr. Muscles had taken a bullet in the chest, but in his case, death seemed to be in order. What goes down comes around.

Anyway, somehow I ended up with a Brother who was getting short and doing mess duty until his rotation came. I think he needed a place to hooch up, and we had an extra cot in the team quarters. I hardly saw the Marine, and for the first week everything was cool.

Then one day we came in off a patrol and went into our quarters to secure our gear. We always kept a tidy hooch, with our weapons stored for easy and quick retrieval. Quang Tri hadn't been the target of much enemy action, but we were always ready. The short-timer's cot was a mess, his weapon was dirty, and his clothes were strewn about. When I inspected his gear, I couldn't find his ammo or grenades. I decided I'd go to debriefing, shower, and then have a talk with Shorty. Just as I was about to leave, he came into the hooch.

"Marine," I said, "you need to clean your weapon and get your stuff squared away."

He didn't respond.

I repeated my words.

He still didn't respond.

"Look," I said, "I'll be back in ten minutes. If you don't get it done, I'll throw your shit out into the company street."

There had been a downpour, and the company street was muddy. I sloshed up to the company office to mail a letter, planning to give the guy plenty of time to respond. I visited with Ernie for a bit and then returned to the hooch. Shorty was gone, and he hadn't touched a thing.

I picked up his cot with all his gear and threw it into the street. It landed in the mud and tipped over. About an hour later he came strolling back to the hooch. We had words. He left his stuff in the street and disappeared again. I figured he had gone to get help, so I slammed a clip in my M-16 and sat on my cot. Sure enough, he came back with the biggest Marine I'd ever seen. I had seen this guy packing the M-60, and he made the gun look like a toy. He stood at least 6 foot 8, and his biceps rippled.

I knew the story. The big guy would hammer me for picking on the short-timer. It had become a conflict of black against white. I wasn't going to go hand to hand with this overgrown slab of muscle. I knew my physical science well enough to understand that for every action there is an equal and opposite reaction, and this big guy could very easily mop the floor with me. If he did, the little guy would get away with his act of defiance.

I slammed a round in the chamber.

"I will waste you both," I said. There was no doubt in my mind that I would pull the trigger.

They stopped in their tracks.

"All you have to do is get your shit squared away. It's that simple." I spoke evenly, gripping the rifle.

The big guy flared his nostrils, backed off, and tried to stare me down. I sat ready in silence. The last thing I wanted to do was to cut loose with a full auto burst and shoot my countrymen. The standoff lasted about five minutes. Finally the big guy left. I must have looked wild-eyed and crazy enough to convince them that I would carry out my threat.

Shorty began picking up his gear. He cleaned his weapon and did his laundry.

Fragging hadn't come to recon yet, but I feared I might be the first. The perfect murder weapon is the hand grenade. It leaves no fingerprints and no clues as to who tossed it. The problem was big and dangerous, and I went to the gunny and told him the whole story.

"Put him on point until he goes home," the gunny said.

"On point? I don't even want him near me, let alone in the bush with me. He could waste me in the rear."

"He won't do anything," the gunny said. "He's not the type."

I hoped the gunny knew this Marine better than I did. I asked him to send Shorty to another team.

"If I do that, he'll know he intimidates you," the gunny replied.

There was a short pause as the gunny and I looked each other in the eye. I wasn't sure why he was taking the position he was. Then I asked, "What about the big guy?"

"I'll keep an eye on him."

This was not good. I'd already proven to myself that I couldn't sleep with one eye open. The gunny had to sleep too. It would be very easy for either of these Marines to toss a grenade into the hooch and blow me into the land of the wasted.

The whole incident disturbed me to the bone. I would never have thought that I would have to threaten a fellow Marine, much less fear for my life at the hand of one. It was the pits to fear your countrymen as much as you did the NVA. If I'd been forced to pull the trigger, who knows what would have happened? I could have spent the rest of my life in prison.

I told the team the situation and advised them to sleep with other teams. I would be bunker hopping for a spell.

"Make sure all of your grenades are in your pack, and keep your pack with you," I said. It would be too easy to borrow a grenade.

The team helped me watch Shorty until he finally rotated out. The big guy never came near me, and about two weeks after the incident, he disappeared. Apparently he didn't like our lifestyle and had decided to desert. Word came back that he had been picked up in Da Nang and would do some jail time. I was one happy guy to have both of them gone for good.

I could sleep again, but after that I always had a nagging feeling that a grenade could come rolling in as I slept. When fragging did finally reach us, however, I wasn't the target.

When Sergeant Johnson left, we got a staff sergeant who always seemed to get up on the wrong side of the cot. I don't know if he felt that we were just a bunch of kids who didn't know our rectums from our rifles, but he seemed to be constantly trying to find things that were wrong or things for us to do. I think he was a Korean vet, and it would be my guess that the generation gap was just a little too wide for him. Or maybe his home life was miserable and he was taking it out on us. What really bugged us was that we were doing our jobs. Every patrol operated to the high standards demanded by the task at hand. We were running missions back to back, and the last thing we needed was some nitpicky lifer making our lives miserable between missions.

Although we never talked about it, it was interesting that Marines with the rank of E-5 (sergeant) or below commanded most of the missions. I personally never went on patrol with an officer or anyone above the rank of E-5, and to be honest, I liked it that way. I never saw Grumpy go out, and it was probably a good thing that he hung out in the rear, because after a month of several cases of borderline insubordination with the old grouch, someone got his belly full.

The sergeant was entering the hooch when the explosion rattled the company street. The blast teetered him backwards, but he managed to remain standing. The screen door hung smoking in his hand; the rest of the hooch lay on the ground. The person who planted the charges was an expert, so it wasn't attempted murder, but if he had been caught, there would have been hell to pay. No matter the reason, it wasn't acceptable to go around blowing up things or people on the company street.

A serious investigation ensued. Our team had the perfect alibi: We had been in the bush. They tried to find a team with C-4 explosives that were unaccounted for, but it was a futile effort because up to this point there had been little control over how many explosives we carried. In every team's hooch there was just about everything needed to wage war: grenades, M-16s, C-4s, smoke grenades, tear gas grenades—you name it. We were heavily armed and not counting.

Grumpy was transferred out of the company the day of the explosion. Not a soul hated to see him go. Most of us simply wouldn't put up with being hassled. The bush harassed us enough, and we had a pretty good handle on the difference between our rectums and our rifles.

The difficulties of military combat are not limited to the battlefield. Choppers malfunction and fall from the sky, jeeps flip over, and weapons accidentally discharge. Just walking from point A to point B can be deadly. Such was the case for Tomás A. Barrera.

LZ Stud was a hub that recon Marines were inserted from or came back to after a mission. Barrera and his team were either coming or going to LZ Stud when disaster struck. Walking along a partially submerged footbridge to cross a swollen stream, the men were holding on to ropes to steady themselves as they crossed the water. Laden with the heavy radio, Tomás somehow lost his grip, fell into the stream, and disappeared. George Stuber immediately jumped into the fast-moving water and nearly drowned in his unsuccessful attempts to find his friend. Barrera's body was found a few days later, and George was awarded the Navy/Marine Corps Medal for his valiant effort to save Tomás.

George was one of those Marines who had some trouble following all of the rules. Apparently he would go AWOL from time to time, and each time he did, the clock would start over again on his enlistment. George was reportedly on year number five of his two-year enlistment when the Corps decided to discharge him under less than honorable conditions. It was another case of a Marine who, even though he wasn't exactly the squared-a-way type, wouldn't hesitate to risk his life to save a fellow Marine. Death and courage of the highest order can show up together just about anywhere, anytime. The general who had presented George with his medal saw to it that he was honorably discharged.

After this incident Ernie was in a black mood. After some gentle prodding, he finally told me that he had mentioned to Barrera that he should find and install some quick release straps for his web gear. It was apparent that both the radioman in Oki and Barrera had drowned because the weight of their radio had sucked them down.

Man has copied his camouflage, yet no man has been able to replicate his soft, padded paw and ability to move noiselessly in the bush. With front teeth as deadly as bayonets and eyesight that can spot a mouse at 200 yards, this big cat can ambush its prey and kill it with a speed and stealth that we humans can only hope to imitate.

One day a team from Charlie Company was carrying out a relatively uneventful mission near the Laotian border. The NVA didn't seem to be about, and after a long morning of sneaking and scouring their RZ, the team stopped for a break. They assumed the standard defensive posture, and some of the men snoozed while at least two stood watch. All was quiet, very quiet.

The tiger could smell the Marines before he could see them, and their smell made his stomach growl. The human conflict in his hunting grounds had made food difficult to come by, and it had been too long since he'd had a good meal. The cat quietly stalked toward the prey lying concealed in the vegetation. Today he would devour a two-legged creature, not as meaty as a deer, but food was food, even if it did smell different than his regular prey. The cat hunkered down and made ready to spring.

There was no warning, no rustle in the bush—just screams of pain and fear as the tiger caught the young Marine in his jaws and dragged him away for consumption. The team sprang into action, giving chase to the tiger, whose sharp teeth held their friend by the neck.

The radio back at battalion headquarters vibrated with the harsh noise of rifle fire in the background as they received the report. The radioman's request for immediate extraction was forwarded to the air wing, and choppers were immediately dispatched to pick up the team.

Well-placed rounds had brought the tiger down. As he quivered and died, the tiger rolled over, released his viselike grip, and let the Marine slip from his jaws. The team administered the best first aid they could for their bloodied friend, who had severe wounds to the neck. They hoped the choppers would arrive quickly. The jungle silence had been broken, and they were compromised.

The choppers landed without incident, the team loaded the wounded Marine and the tiger, and they all flew back to Quang Tri. The 300-pound cat was hung up and skinned. The word was that the skin would be sent to the Marine who had nearly become lunch.

A week or so later not far from where the team had its encounter, a tiger killed a grunt Marine. The NVA, snakes, leeches, and mosquitoes already contested the bush. Now on every mission we would wonder if we were being stalked by the best in the business. One more reason to sleep with one eye open—or not to sleep at all.

There were two corpsmen that served with us on several missions. They were good friends, and one of them was about to rotate home. On his last night in Nam, he procured some booze so he could celebrate with his friend. Sometime in the night the two decided to hold a quick-draw contest with their 45 pistols.

I still remember the ring of the shot. The whole area came alive. Gunfire in the night brings everyone to his feet. In the dark of night, one of the corpsmen lay dead with a 45 slug in his chest. The other had forgotten to unload his pistol before the contest, and now he stood weeping over the body of his friend. One corpsmen would go home in a bag; the other would go to prison. It was a sad ending to honorable service with our unit and a bad day for two families waiting for their men to get home.

Death had come again with a hooded face. There were too many ways to die here.

On one mission, Meatball and his team stumbled into a large force of NVA. An intense fight ensued as they ran for high ground, small arms fire chasing them every step of the way. Huffing and puffing from the weight of his gear in the hot afternoon, the radioman was yelling for an emergency extraction. Meatball knew his team was in dire straits. If the choppers didn't arrive ASAP, his team would probably get wasted. Again the life and death of a team depended on the hammering blades.

Soon the airwaves crackled with the sounds of a savior overhead, and the Army Huey dropped in under heavy fire. The door gunners let fly their firepower, while Meatball and his team cranked out as much fire as they could as they scampered into the bird. Following normal procedures, the radioman was the last one to clamber aboard, but this time the chopper lifted off before he was inside.

Yelling as loud as he could, Meatball told the pilot to set back down. The pilot kept going up. Seeing that he was going to get left, the radioman dove for the skids of the Huey. Wrapping his arms around a skid, he held it in a death grip. Furious, Meatball kept hollering for the pilot to set back down, but the bird continued to climb out of the hot zone. Seeing that the pilot was not going to set down, Meatball concentrated on trying to get the radioman aboard. He knew the heavy pack would strain the radioman to the limit and that if they didn't get him aboard quickly, they would lose him to the jungle floor. They lowered a rope to him, but the prop wash and air currents kept it dangling out of his reach. Meatball screamed again for the pilot to set down, but the bird kept going up.

The G forces against the radioman were winning, and the last thing Meatball and the team saw before the radioman lost his grip was the fear in his eyes. From 1500 feet he tumbled to his death. When the chopper landed, the team had to restrain Meatball to keep him from killing the pilot.

When the team got back to Quang Tri, I sat with Meatball and we talked. Still full of rage, he told me that even though the small-arms fire had been intense, there hadn't been any reason for the pilot not to set back down. They had flown over several LZs, any one of which would have given the radioman a chance to get inside.

"The cowardly son of a bitch killed him," he said.

Word came back to Echo Company that the incident would be investigated. The unofficial rumor was that the pilot was new to Nam and hadn't been in a hot LZ before. All of us scoffed at that. We had seen too many brave pilots who had never touched the throttle until all of us were accounted for. It had been a terrible, needless waste of a good radioman, a good Marine.

The next day a team went out to recover the radioman's body. They found him impaled in the trees. He had died alone as the chopper continued its climb.

Ernie, Meatball, and I sat waiting solemnly for the recovery team to return. I suppose at least one of us should have shed some tears, but all three pumps were still jammed. Although we had become brothers of blood, the bond was loose. Each of us had become little islands unto ourselves. This island was the well of our souls, the pit of our emotions, the part of us we didn't even acknowledge to ourselves, much less to each other. The cement of our bonds allowed each to depend on the other in a fight or an emergency, but the bond didn't extend to our wells. We could not—would not—allow anyone close enough to hear the rocks splash inside our beings.

Ernie had lost several friends who were radiomen. He looked me in the eye and said, "If I die, bury me facedown so the whole world can kiss my ass." After a spell he got up, kicked something in the hooch, and walked outside.

Death was still around, and it kept delivering souls to a place we could not see.

One time "Doc" Sid Rosser joined Tut and Ernie's team on a mission into an area that had seen several contests between reconners and the NVA. As usual, it was good to have a corpsman along in case of a medical emergency. Although the first few days of the mission were quiet, Tut and Ernie sensed that trouble could be just around the next bush.

It was, and in this case, the medical emergency was Sid's. On the third day he apparently sat on a snake. The strike was swift, and the fang marks provided positive proof that he was in trouble. The team requested an emergency extraction, and it was approved—but only for Doc.

It was a decision that only some noncombatant could have made. When he told me about the incident, Ernie said, "I couldn't believe they'd send in a chopper and then make the rest of the team stay in the bush."

Intending to follow the asinine orders, Ernie threw Sid over his back and packed him to a landing zone a few hundred yards to their north. Acting as the pack mule kept Doc's system calm and decreased the flow of venom. When the team reached the LZ, they spotted some movement. The NVA had found them and were maneuvering toward them. Ernie had to run back and retrieve his radio. As he made his dash, the team came under fire at the LZ. He was on his way back to it when the chopper dropped in. Running harder now, he tripped and fell on his face. The rest of the team had gotten aboard, and the chopper's engine began to race as the pilot prepared to lift off.

Tut saw Ernie struggling to get back on his feet and ran back to help him up. When the chopper's engine continued to race, a Marine drew a 45 pistol and placed it against the pilot's head to make sure the chopper made no vertical movement until Tut and Ernie were aboard. A screaming match ensued. The pilot was very upset about having a gun to his head, and the copilot was even madder. To make matters worse, the incoming fire was intensifying. With small-arms fire chasing them, Tut and Ernie raced for the chopper. Once they were inside, the Marine removed the 45 from the pilot's head.

The team arrived safely at Quang Tri. Doc was treated for the snakebite. The snake must not have been poisonous, because Doc returned to duty a couple of days later. There was a big stink about the pistol-to-the-head incident, and the Marine was threatened with court martial. Of course, the pilot said that he wasn't going to leave Tut and Ernie. But after what happened to Meatball's radioman, no one was taking chances with any pilot who gave the slightest hint that he was going to leave someone on the ground.

For two days the reconners had struggled through the dense jungle, picking their way through the thick, snarled vegetation. So far the team hadn't seen the enemy, and the enemy hadn't seen them. It was looking like just another mission where Charlie was not around and the jungle was going to be the meanest adversary.

The triple canopy let very little sunshine down to the jungle floor, making it seem like a thick fog bank where it's impossible to see more than a few feet ahead of you. Working its way in the fog, the team was shocked to suddenly find a spotter plane nose-down in the dirt. Easing along the fuselage, one of the team members peeked through the front windshield.

The eyeless skull startled him. The remains of the pilot sat in solitude, still strapped in the seat of his plane. The flight helmet sat loosely on his skull and the safety belt lay slack against his skeleton. The jungle had done its dirty work. The bones had been picked clean of all flesh and blood. The man had died alone, hopefully before his plane hit the ground.

The Marine reached in and pulled his dog tags, and the team left his bones to rest in peace in the hot green cemetery.

The grunts had their latrines; we had a two-holer. It was a decent-sized structure, with a roof large enough to hold at least two Marines. We liked to hoodwink new guys into spending a night on the roof to stand "rocket watch."

The night they blasted Echo Company with the incoming, there was a new guy lying on the roof of the latrines. Later he related the fearful experience of lying up there and having the rockets scream in.

"Why didn't you get in a bunker?" someone asked.

The dedicated Marine said that General Orders stated he must never leave his post.

We all laughed at his dedication, but inside we were glad that the poor soul hadn't been blown away. It would have been a difficult letter for the commanding officer to draft. How do you tell the family of a dead Marine that their loved one was wasted while lying on the roof of the latrines?

One morning a Marine stumbled down the street to do his business. Throwing the door open, he was so surprised at what he saw that he stumbled backwards.

"Come on in," two feminine, round-eyed voices taunted the totally befuddled Marine. We had no idea that a troop of entertainers had shown up, and even entertainers must answer the call of Mother Nature. The unsuspecting Marine nearly had a cardiac arrest.

So many ways to die, so hard to stay alive.

11
INTO THE VALLEY OF THE SHADOW

In early May 1969 teams from other companies were continually bumping into Charlie and taking casualties. In Echo Company, Tut's team seemed to be getting all the action. Mac and I, on the other hand, made several missions but came up empty-handed. We kept wondering when we would find Charlie—or when he would find us.

Then we were picked for a mission into the dreaded A Shau. During the briefing, we were told that a major operation was going to take place and that recon teams were going in ahead of the grunts to scout for them. Foot soldiers didn't grow old in the A Shau. Out there somewhere were the rotting corpses of dead reconners who had fallen in one of the many fights in that haunted valley.

When I became a team leader, I'd been excited about being in command and thought I was both capable and mentally ready to fill the slot. But as time went on, I felt increasingly anxious. My confidence level was still high, but I missed being with Tut, Ernie, and Meatball. My team was not as experienced as our original group. I was also getting short again, and it seemed that no matter how many missions we went on, no matter how many NVA our little bands spotted or killed, we still paid a heavy price for snooping around in Charlie country.

Deep down, I was also questioning this war. Having gone out on twenty-some long-range missions and I don't know how many grunt patrols, I couldn't see much evidence that things were getting better. The war seemed to drag on with no real attempt to end the carnage. Fortunately, my missions were going okay, but my own mortality was haunting me, and at times I felt I had just about outlived my good fortune. It was weird. I think I really realized that I was living on borrowed time. I also understood that I had developed a love-hate relationship with the bush. I wanted to be where the action was, but I was becoming more and more anxious about the price tag. I guess it was like waiting for the hammer to hit the anvil. I knew it was suspended, but I didn't know when it was going to fall.

I noticed that my throat was a little tighter every time I waited for the choppers. This tension grew just a little each time, and after I took the reins of a team, I felt even more ill at ease. While we were waiting for an insertion, I would look around the team and hope I could—would—honor them with the leadership they deserved. Their lives and their futures depended on how I reacted to situations in the bush. I didn't enjoy this responsibility, and waiting for the hammer to fall wasn't a good feeling.

We painted our faces, checked our gear, and got ready for the insertion. The topo maps indicated brutal terrain. Mac thought we should bring along at least one LAW, and I agreed. We wanted to travel light because of the terrain, but we also wanted to be as heavily armed as possible. Once again we carefully balanced the gear we needed to sustain life with what we needed to take it.

The choppers dropped us off in the middle of a grunt company so we could talk to the commanding officer before we went into the valley. It had been a long time since I'd been around grunts. When we walked into the perimeter from the LZ, we were met with curious stares. It never occurred to me that the grunts had seen little of recon teams. I suppose the painted faces, along with the absence of helmets and flack jackets, did make us look quite different.

The captain in command seemed happy to see us. Mac and I went with him to discuss the mission while the rest of the team sat down and waited for us to return. The captain unfolded his maps and pointed out his areas of interest. He showed us where some blocking forces were set and gave us a brief overview of the upcoming operation. Our recon zone would be the right flank of his forces, and he wanted to know what was out there.

"Well," I said, as if it were just another mission, "We'll go in and find out."

No one knew how apprehensive I really was. I've never been big on premonitions, yet I had a nagging feeling that we were heading into trouble. The terrain we had just flown over was deadly looking. The ridges were steep, the canyons deep. The canopy looked like it hid a ghostly forest where a guy could run into the headless horseman. This was without question one place where you didn't want to confuse your rectum with your rifle.

We finished the talk with the CO and walked back to the LZ. The team got up and followed us. The choppers would come as soon as they could, and we would be inserted. While we waited, we laughed and joked among ourselves. I suppose we were showing off a bit for the solemn grunts sitting in foxholes above the landing zone.

It was a good cover. No one could see how tense I really was.

"Check your gear," I said. The assertion of authority eased the strain on my nerves.

We busied ourselves checking our weapons and water and looking for potential sources of noise. Everything had to hang just right, so it wouldn't make any noise. The radiomen checked the radios, and I stood up to give the team a once over. They were a brave lot. This little band of eight men with green-and-black painted faces would go anywhere they were asked to go. Without complaint, they would step off choppers deep into country miles away from the closest friendly forces. They would, one step at a time, walk into areas that could be crawling with people who wanted them dead.

The wild winds created by the Huey blades kicked up the dirt and anything else not fastened down by nature, and we hopped aboard for the short flight to our RZ. As we rose above the perimeter, I waved to a gawking grunt. He just looked at me. I smiled my bravest smile, and he returned some kind of smirk. Who knows what he was thinking?

There was something awesome about hammering along above the jungle before an insertion. Knowing we would soon set foot on Charlie's turf, our adrenaline reached its highest octane. It was a mix of boiling blood and fear of the unknown. Would Charlie be waiting for us at the LZ? Would he allow us to land and then when the choppers were gone, open up and turn us into shredded Marines? Or would the chopper take too much lead and come crashing down, with its blades bending and cutting at us like a swinging guillotine? Every time my foot hit the ground, I expected a hail of fire to hit us. When it didn't happen, the oxygen would fill my lungs, and the adrenaline would race through my veins, boosting my courage.

We flew over two ridges east of the entrenched grunts. The terrain still bothered me, but there was nothing to do but live through the insertion, get out of the chopper, and do our business. We dropped into an LZ surrounded by steep ridges and eerie dark green vegetation. It looked as if napalm had been here before us. The Huey maneuvered around a big burnt snag and set down. We bailed off like we always did: The radioman was first off, the team leader hit the ground right behind the radioman, and the rest of the team followed.

As the chopper lifted, we lay prostrate in a circle around the LZ for a few moments, just long enough to see if we would get hit. If we did, the choppers were still close enough to come back and get us out. I looked around again, and suddenly I felt like a little plastic toy soldier who had been dropped off on another planet. What was it that Sun Tzu had said? *Wherever the road is difficult to negotiate, it is entrapping terrain.* That was it. Everywhere I looked, entrapping terrain surrounded us.

Mac must have seen it in my eyes. He looked at me and shook his head sideways. I tried not to let the team see my worry lines.

There was no incoming, so we immediately stood up, formed a column, and moved about two hundred yards north, where the landscape dove off into a steep draw. We had to go down deep before we could go up. I knew this would make it almost impossible to maintain good communications, so I asked the radioman to get a radio check.

He confirmed my suspicion. "I can barely hear the CP," he said. "They're breaking up."

I didn't want to go any further without radio contact. The place was without a doubt the dark side of the moon, and if we got into a fight, I knew we would need all the help we could get. The terrain was so bad that if

Charlie was around, all he had to do was swarm down on us. If he had manglers with him, he could simply bomb us from above. I now understood how a bug encircled by the leaves of a Venus flytrap might feel.

I gave a hand signal to halt the team, and we immediately formed a defensive perimeter to our front. My plan was to string a claymore wire in a tree to see if it would enable us to communicate clearly with the CP. If so, we could continue the penetration with some confidence of getting help if we needed it.

"Hand me your wire," I whispered to the assistant radioman.

The crosshairs of the rifle sights must have met dead center on the radioman's head. As he turned to grasp the wire, a shot broke the silence, and the dirt in front of the team came alive as bullets kicked the earth and grass around us. A round whizzed by my head. I looked down at the radioman. He was lying on his back with his eyes wide open, and I was sure he was dead. When he blinked his eyes, a flood of relief surged through my boiling blood. His right eyebrow was missing but, thank God, he was all right.

Laughing almost insanely, I fired back at our unseen enemy along with the rest of the team. I was so thankful that there was no bullet hole between the radioman's eyes that my relief came out in my voice. In a giddy tone, I yelled for the team to leapfrog back to the LZ. We had to climb back up to a little knoll next to it, where the higher ground would provide better fighting terrain. One by one we laid down a base of fire and peeled backwards. The incoming fire was intense.

We made it back to the LZ without taking any casualties. I yelled for a ceasefire to conserve ammo and told Mac to spread the team out in line and find the best cover possible for defense. I was amazed at our good fortune. The elevation of the gunner's mark had been perfect for a shot right between the radioman's running lights. If he hadn't turned his head at the precise moment he had, he would have been shot quite dead. And if the gunner had held his elevation, he would have hit at least four of us. Maybe we had stepped into an NVA boot camp and their new guys were still learning to shoot. At any rate, this time the hammer missed the anvil.

I hollered for the assistant radioman to call for an extraction and some artillery and then told the radioman to let me take another look at his head. Someone lobbed a grenade down the hill, and another Marine followed with two more. After the explosions, the team lit up cigarettes. No one was concerned about dying of lung cancer.

"Damn, that was a close call," I said to the radioman.

He wiped his hand across the missing brow and cracked a thin smile. Then he said, "I left the radio. I'll go back and get it." I hadn't noticed that the radio was missing, so the radioman's remark threw me for a loop. I told him that the radio wasn't worth getting killed over. That decision would later cost me, but for now the radio was forgotten.

Mac had spotted a bunker complex on top of the tall ridge on our right flank. All he could see through the binoculars was the top of one bunker, but we had learned that where there was one bunker, there were always more. Bunkers seemed to breed and give birth to full-grown offspring that were home to mean little yellow men.

Our secondary radio was communicating okay, but there were still breakups. The sound of an approaching plane boosted our spirits.

"South Side, this is Bird Dog 3." The voice on the radio was jovial and had a Spanish accent. Our Don Quixote had arrived.

The OV-10 came flying in, and once again we had excellent communications. Suddenly, a burst of fire went off.

"Movement below," Mac hollered.

As the team filled the vegetation full of holes, I took the handset from the assistant radioman and asked the pilot to lay down some fire directly in front of us.

"No problem, man," the pilot said.

A Willie-Peter marker round hit beyond the cover of the advancing foes. I had no idea if there were two or two hundred of them. I told the pilot to drop 50 meters and let them have it.

I wanted to pray that no manglers would bracket us from the bunker above. I couldn't pray. All I could do was talk to the pilot and hope he could buy us some time with his fire.

The pilot calmed my fears. He talked as if he and his Rocinante were on a Sunday ride with us. His voice was comical, but his piloting was exceptional. On one pass the Hispanic fool made a low-level barrel roll and then asked me to critique his rollover.

Through the glasses, Mac saw hurried movement on the ridge where the bunker sat.

"Give them a blast with the LAW!" I said.

Mac didn't hesitate, and I told the pilot what we were shooting at.

"Gotcha," he said.

The LAW round landed just below the bunker. We couldn't tell if it killed the grass or the gooks.

"Choppers are on the way," the pilot radioed. "Arty's coming too. Keep your heads down."

The 155s smashed into the hill above and the draw below, laying down a ring of fire. The sound of a freight train coming in with that deadly end-over-end sound was always good, savage music. The artillery was smashing in so close that we covered our heads with our packs. Two Ch-46s flew overhead, and it looked as though we were about to get out of this potentially fatal terrain.

Then the radio crackled with the news that the birds were low on fuel and wouldn't be coming down to pluck us out.

"Man, if they don't get us out of here before nightfall, we are dead men," someone on the team remarked.

It was getting late, and his remark was truer than any of us wanted to admit.

"Check your ammo and grenades." I spoke with the calmest voice I could find. I felt like a rubber band stretching and stretching, but I didn't want the twanging vibration to show up in my voice.

We lay watching for any signs of movement. We maintained good fire discipline, conserving ammo, but the minute anything rustled, we turned it into Swiss cheese. Our ammo level was about 70 percent, so we could sustain a good fight if we had to. Our main objective, however, was to get some choppers in here to get us out.

Another pair of choppers flew over, but reports of mechanical trouble again dashed our hopes. Was our location so spooky that these guys would just leave us here? Maybe they had the same thoughts I did. This place looked like the devil's second home. Just looking at it made my skin crawl. All we needed was one chopper to drop in—all we needed was one little bird with wings that worked.

Silence... There was an awful hush out there, just beyond our little stand. I asked our rear guard if he saw anything. There was a long pause. I couldn't see him, so I worried that he had been hit and was dead.

"No movement," he whispered at last.

Arty came pounding in again and broke the silence.

We tossed a couple of grenades into some tall grass. It could have been the wind causing the grass to sway, but if it was, the wind died in the explosions.

Finally the radio crackled, and some smart ass asked if we were waiting for a taxi. This was one of those times when things were so tense that you thought you could hear your brain sizzling, and as usual, there was some joker who broke the tension with a remark that almost made you laugh.

"Roger," I replied. "We'd like a ride out of this hole."

I was concerned that the CH-46 would have a hard time landing on the small LZ. I sent two guys out to see if they could push the burnt stump over, but they couldn't, and they rushed back, sweating from the endeavor. I called the chopper.

"Watch out for that stump in the middle of the LZ!"

"Roger, we see it."

Bury Me With Soldiers

The bird swooped in, flew backwards, and missed the stump. The tailgate lowered, and we ran for the bowels of the mechanical bird. Mac was the first to hit the ramp, and as soon as he was inside, he swung his rifle butt at the windows like a madman killing snakes. Each of us stuck our weapon out a hole and cranked fire. The door gunner joined in the rat-tat-tat with his heavy gun.

The liftoff felt better than not dying a virgin.

We landed back at the grunt perimeter with about twenty minutes of light left. The door gunner motioned to me that the pilot wanted to talk to me, so I stepped out of the bird and waited for him. If he wanted a kiss, I would be glad to plant one on his cheek. The pilot walked up to me with a cigarette hanging loosely from his lips. He was not smiling.

"Damn you guys," he said. "Every time I pluck you Marines out of trouble, you break my windows." The cigarette danced in angry time to the pilot's moving lips.

I was taken aback by his mood. I was very happy to be alive and still coming down off the high-octane rush. I almost locked up and had trouble finding words. Then,. with my eyes fixed on his face, I let slip a smile.

"Sir, that was a damn good piece of flying you just did," I said. "You must have balls as big as my dad's registered Angus bull back home on the ranch."

The pilot's eyes drifted sideways to meet mine, and a very thin smile showed up on his face. I knew I had him.

The pilot walked up the tailgate, shaking his head. When no one else could see him, he gave me the finger across his head in an obscene, mock salute. His smile was much broader now. I smiled and let out a laugh. It had taken some testicles to drop in on us when things were hot, and he knew it. He also knew that he had saved our lives and that he would get new windows for the next recon team in trouble. I wished I had read his nametag.

The next order of business was to find the captain and tell him about the radio. I knew it would be bad news for him to hear and even worse news for me to deliver. I braced myself for a butt chewing, court martial, and loss of my stripes.

The captain's face fell when I told him that the radio was still out in the bush. He told the colonel, and the colonel told the captain, who told the corporal (that would be me) that the radio must be recovered. The corporal told the captain to tell the colonel that it was crazy to go back there for anything, much less a radio. The captain, with his lips tight, told the corporal that the colonel had said what the captain expected and that the corporal had damn well better do what the colonel wanted. (This is a fine example of what we called communicating through the chain of command.)

I knew I had fouled up by not charging down that draw to get the radio. I also knew that my team had gotten back with only one minor wound. I told the captain I would go out in the morning to get the radio. Then if I had any gonads left, I would go tell the colonel what I thought about his radio—and this whole damn war to boot.

I didn't sleep well that night. It isn't easy to go to sleep when there's an upset grunt colonel nearby. Today hadn't gone well. I hadn't lost any men, and that gave me some comfort. Leaving the radio had been a snap decision, and I knew that if I or anyone else had gone after it, there would have been blood on the jungle floor. A dead or wounded man would have compounded our situation. Still, I felt that I had failed.

As I reflected on the day's action, it seemed to me to have been a stroke of good fortune that we had had trouble with the radio in the first place. If we had continued walking, there was no shred of doubt that we would have been funneled into an ambush. The terrain would have led us right into it. A movement in any direction would have been fatal. Today had been a mixture of good and not so good. I laid my head back and again tried to sleep. My right ear still rang from the bullet cracking by. I longed for the sound of squeaky leather.

Sometime in the middle of the night I decided that I would go out on one more mission and then ask for a job in the rear. The bush was getting to me. I no longer felt invincible, and the nagging thought of not getting out of Vietnam alive was intensifying. I thought it would be a big fat miracle if I lived through tomorrow. It occurred to me that this was how an inmate must feel on the night before his execution.

After I finally fell asleep, I wished I had stayed awake. Dreaming about smiling little yellow men hovering over the radio kept me on the edge of the cliff all night. This dream was a little different than the one where they had me suspended over the cliff with the viper pit at the bottom. In this dream a little canary yellow man jumped out at me and started a fight. He wasn't armed; it was a fistfight he wanted. He called me dirty names and told me I wasn't fit to fight his comrades. I began swinging, but I couldn't connect my fist with his head. The yellow man didn't even duck. It was as if my arms were too short to reach him and my feet were staked to the ground. He just stood there and let me exhaust myself. When I was played out like a fish on a line, he grabbed me and bound my hands. Thank God, I jolted awake.

When morning finally came, I wasn't tired, but I was full of anxiety. I didn't want to go back into the headless horseman's forest. The colonel told the captain to tell the corporal to get on the LZ. The team, the captain, and the corporal all went to the LZ, per the colonel's orders. The corporal told the team that they would stay at the LZ and the corporal would go get the radio. If all went well, the corporal would be in and out in less than ten minutes.

We landed in exactly the same spot as yesterday, and I bailed off. I suppose I was angry with myself for the decision I'd made yesterday, or maybe I was angry with the colonel, but whatever made me do it, I decided to run for the radio. I wasn't going to be cautious, and I wasn't going to stroll. If I was going to be met with a wall of gunfire, I wanted to run into it and get this life over with. Still, I had a rope in my hand, and if I made it to the radio, I planned to tie the rope to the radio to see if it had been booby-trapped. I would at least take the time to avoid one of Charlie's infamous mauling traps.

I charged for the radio as if it were the end zone. The captain was on my heels all the way. No yellow men were waiting for me, and there was no wall of lead. I don't know if it was a cowardly charge or a courageous charge. The only thing I know was that I was running on the highest octane I'd ever felt. My engine was redlined. If this had been a track meet, nobody could have outrun me—nobody. I felt calm, unafraid, and ready to meet whatever I was to meet. I could outrun fear itself.

I made it to the radio and tied the line. A fast jerk proved that there were no booby traps, so I scooped the radio up and beat feet hard back to the chopper. If fear was still on my trail, it had run past me when I stopped to pick up the radio. I threw the radio into the chopper and then threw myself in headfirst. The captain had to run around the far side to get aboard. I lay on my stomach catching my breath as the bird lifted off.

As soon as we landed with the radio, we got word to saddle up. We had another mission further north, and the choppers were coming to take us back to Quang Tri. It was just as well. I didn't have the gonads to talk to the colonel.

A CH-46 landed, and we clambered aboard. As we climbed away from that haunted valley, I let out a long sigh of relief. I wished our mission had gone better, but I was happy not to have any of my team dead and rotting in that valley of death. I wondered if the colonel had the information he needed. Maybe I should have talked to him, but sometimes it's better to quietly fold your tent and get while the getting is good.

I heard that the operation turned very nasty. I think it became part of the same operation where the Army ended up getting bloodied on Hamburger Hill.

I had made a wise decision to ask for a job in the rear.

12
SHORT-TIMER

Mac and I were about to run our last mission together. With luck, it would be my last.

I'd already spoken to the gunny about getting out of the bush, and he'd said he would find me something to do in the rear. I didn't discuss my fears with him; I just told him that I felt I'd had enough and that it was time to get out. He nodded and told me to check in with him when we got back. In our conversation, I told him that in high school I'd received a B^+ in typing and that all I would need to be a successful Remington raider was about five gallons of whiteout. The gunny looked at me a little funny, so I decided I'd better shut up so I wouldn't confuse him.

Our mission was to take place near the Laotian border. During the initial briefing, we were told that the area had been contested and that Charlie seemed to be using dogs to sniff out recon teams in the area. It sounded as if we might find some dog poop to hammer.

The mission was bad from the get-go. When the chopper landed during our insertion, a booby trap went off, and we were shot out of the LZ. The NVA had picked a good place to set its trap; there weren't many LZs in that neck of the woods. We took no casualties and returned to base for another shot at it the next day. After today's experience, finding a place to insert was going to be a challenge.

I was, without question, on pins and thorns. Bad luck always seemed to show up when a guy was getting close to going home. The "last mission" always seemed to go awry. There had been more than one Marine wasted on his last trip into the jungle. Though I was nervous, I wasn't going to let fear chase me out of the jungle with my tail between my legs. I was ready to get out of the bush, but I wouldn't let the bush run me out. I figured that whatever would be, would be. Besides, I had the good name of Elmer Fudd to uphold, and no cwazy wabbit was going to get the best of me.

The day after the failed insertion, we were picked up and flown into the RZ. I was crawling with feelings of apprehension, which I ignored and hopefully concealed. As we hammered along, the pilot of one of the gunships kept asking me where I wanted to insert. Every single LZ looked dangerous. I wanted some high ground, but it appeared that all of the LZs were sitting on the low terrain. The pilot was becoming impatient with me, and I was becoming irritated with him. We almost got into a shouting match over the radio. I wasn't going in until I found the right LZ.

Banking hard to the left, the Huey groaned against the air. I saw a little knob that rose slightly above a canyon. I pointed down, and we fell out of the sky rapidly. We bailed out and made our way for cover.

"Finally!" The pilot's agitated voice came over the radio.

I wanted to tell the jerk to come down here with us, spend a few nights, and see how he liked it. Unlike him, we wouldn't be going to the officers' club tonight for a cold beer. It was the only time I didn't find a pilot personable. Maybe this guy was getting short and testy also. Whatever was going on, we were glad to be rid of each other. He flew away and we humped along. Someone in the team stuck his finger high in the air to tell the cranky pilot how we felt about his lack of respect.

The rest of the day went okay. We moved carefully and methodically. My point man was very good at picking his way in the bush. He always kept us high enough to avoid entrapment and low enough to stay off the skyline. About thirty minutes before dark we set up a temporary night harbor. Then after dark I moved the team about 100 meters to some high ground for the night, a feint I hoped would make us harder to find in the dark.

Night came and we stood our designated watches. For some reason, I felt really fatigued and fell into a very deep sleep. In the middle of the night I was rousted. Moving lights had been spotted below us. I raised up but couldn't get my eyes to focus. Flopping back down, I mumbled, "Call it in and let me know if they get any closer." I don't know why I reacted that way. I should have bolted awake and called in Arty. I guess bone weariness had me in its grip, because I couldn't have cared less that the enemy was moving about. Whatever the reason, I slept until it was my turn for watch.

Daylight came, and we sat for a spell to see if Charlie was still down there. All was quiet. I finally decided that we would sneak on down and see if we could find out what was going on. The cover was good, so I figured we could get closer for the inspection.

We picked our way down to a small draw. I don't know who scared whom the most. We never saw them, but the oriental chatter that rose out of the vegetation made my heart skip a few beats. We dove into an old bomb crater and made ready for the fight. We laid on the berm of the crater for a good two hours. Even though the voices disappeared and no attack came, we were almost afraid to move. Finally we slithered out of the crater and made our way to the draw above. From all indications we were in a busy area, and we had to move silently. One mistake and we could be in trouble.

For the next five days we zigzagged the RZ. No other indications of enemy movement were seen or heard. We must have caught the tail end of a unit moving through, and they must have wanted to get out of our RZ without a fight. That suited me just fine. The weather had turned sour, and I was worried about getting support from the choppers.

On day seven the weather was good, and we were notified that we would be picked up soon. The CH-46 set down in our green smoke for what

I hoped would be my last extraction from the bush. I was one very happy short-timer.

After the mission, I told Mac what I was going to do. He nodded his head. I told him he should take the team and become the leader of this pack of homeless men.

"No way," he said, and I didn't blame him.

Mac went to another team. I'm not sure, but I think he transferred to Charlie Company.

About a week later Mac and his five-man team were ambushed. Three men died, and Mac sustained seven AK-47 rounds in his skinny body. When I heard about the attack, I went to the hospital. The choppers had already landed with the two survivors, so I took a seat outside and waited for word on Mac. I was sick. Mac was getting short like the rest of us, and it was a damn shame that he had been shot up so bad. I felt some twinges of responsibility. If I had stayed in the bush, maybe this wouldn't have happened.

Maybe?

After waiting for an hour or so, I got up and decided to find Mac or someone who could tell me what his condition was. There was no one in the ward who could help me, so I began to wander around the hospital. Somehow I made a wrong turn and found myself looking at Mac as they were rolling him over on the operating table. He looked like hamburger. There was torn flesh and blood from his chest to his toes.

A doctor looked up at me, and I looked into his eyes. Our gazes locked in blank stares for a while, and then I turned and went for some air.

Outside I stood numb.

It would be a miracle if Mac lived. It would be a miracle if he wanted to live.

I left the hospital and went to find a bunker. The earth held me again. I didn't know whether to pray for Mac to live or for Mac to die. In any event, I couldn't pray. Something always seemed to block my attempts to talk with God. I think I had finally acknowledged the fact that doing the devil's work made it impossible to be godly. Maybe there was a way to do it, but I never found the path.

I went back the next morning. The ward was full of the wounded. If you ever want to see the horrific ravages of war, go to a field hospital. Mac lay sprawled in a full body cast, with every appendage sticking out. He was a mess, doped to the hilt and in obvious pain. Just as I arrived, a Marine general came in to hand out Purple Hearts. The general laid the medal on the cast covering Mac's chest, stepped back, and saluted him.

Bury Me With Soldiers

Mac returned the salute with his middle finger high in the air.

Oh boy, I thought. *Here's Mac full of holes, and now they're going to court-martial him.*

But the general moved on as if nothing had happened.

It's hard to find words when you're standing in one piece over a chopped up buddy. I found a chair and pulled it up next to his bed.

Mac spoke first. "We were on a damn trail." It hurt him to even talk.

"Is there anything I can do for you?" I asked.

"Get my personal stuff gathered up and shipped home for me."

Later that day, intending to provide some comic relief in a miserable situation, Ernie went to the hospital. He walked into the ward and found Mac.

"I suppose this means you won't pay me back the $20 bucks you borrowed," he said, smiling.

Mac laughed and began coughing. The cough turned to choking and gagging. The pain of any movement hit Mac like a sledgehammer. His eyes rolled back, and he started to slip out of consciousness.

"I thought I killed him," Ernie told me.

It would be almost twenty years before I would learn that Mac was still alive. The spit had come out of the wind and hit him, and Mac had survived it.

For some reason the bridge at Quang Tri became a concern. Apparently the brass were worried that some sneaky yellow man was going to blow it up. I was sent out to the bridge with a team of divers for a daily underwater inspection. A tent had been erected for our stay, and no one was allowed to visit. We were told that we would be here at least a week. Other than being camped close to the outer perimeter, it appeared that it was going to be an easy assignment. I never did understand why we couldn't leave or why others couldn't enter.

Ernie decided to come pay me a visit, but first he had to get past the security on the road to the bridge. He talked a truck driver into letting him lie down in the bed of the truck. It was a pleasant surprise for me to see Ernie rise from his prostrate position in the truck. We walked over to the tent and sat down for a good visit. Ernie told me about going up to Dong Ha for some minor surgery on his hand.

"They strapped my arm to the operating table, and the doc was about to inject the Novocain when I heard the choppers land. Suddenly the place was full of screaming wounded and yelling doctors.

"Someone yelled orders to cut me loose from the table. I stood up just as they placed a bloody Marine on the table. I went out for a smoke and could hear the frantic noises of doctors yelling and the wounded moaning and screaming. It was awful, all that noise.

"About an hour passed and they called me back in. They were still hosing the floor down and picking up body parts from the floor. They strapped me down again and proceeded as if I were the first patient of the day. Man, was I glad to get out of there."

Ernie stayed about an hour. He had to catch the next truck back, and when it pulled up, he made his way over to it and crawled inside to lie down. I thanked him for dropping in and chuckled at the sight of his large frame lying flat in the bed of the truck.

About this time there was a story floating around about a lone NVA soldier who stepped out of the jungle near a major Marine position. Amid the sea of tents, choppers, and Marines, the solitary gunner cranked off a full magazine of ammunition at no particular target. After letting the lead fly, the man turned and walked slowly and defiantly back into the jungle. A team of recon Marines happened to be near enough to witness the event, and they gave the lone gunner a standing ovation.

Maybe the soldier was feeling as frustrated as everyone else and had decided to vent some of his emotions. Whatever caused his outburst, the soldier received full honors from his adversaries.

After the bridge assignment I worked in the company office, filling out my days typing the company diary. I was also sent out a couple of times to make some dives. On one dive we were looking for underwater ammo caches. I was a bit nervous because just a week earlier a diver had been shot dead in the water.

One day I was told to get to the LZ with my diving gear. The word was that a Navy boat had been blown apart on the river. Two men were missing, and several cases of mortar rounds lay on the bottom of the river. It felt really odd to be sitting at the LZ with scuba gear and no weapon. A heavily armed recon team sat around me with painted faces. I felt nude without a rifle or grenades or paint on my face, and my diving partner looked as naked as I felt. Those short-timer feelings were also nagging at me. I had thought my last mission with Mac would be my last visit to Charlie country.

The plan was to chopper up to the place where Charlie had attacked the boat. My partner and I would get in the water, look for the bodies of the men, and then recover the munitions off the river bottom. From the sounds of things, it was going to be a grisly task. I thought about telling the CO that

I was too short to be swimming around in Charlie-infested waters, but I just sat on the LZ and waited, trying not to think.

After a couple of hours of waiting, the radio crackled with the news that the mission had been scrubbed. I picked up my diving gear and headed back to the company area, happy to have the mission canceled. I didn't really like the thought of going out without a weapon in my hand. And I really didn't like the thought of stuffing body parts into a green bag.

To this day I don't understand why I did it, but I told Tut that if he got any good missions, I would go out with him. It was without question the dumbest thing I have ever said, especially because I didn't properly define the word *good*.

One night when I had less than two weeks to go before I was out of there, Tut shook me awake at 0200 hours and told me to grab my gear and get to the LZ. The rain was coming down hard in a steady hammering and sideways flow that beat hard against the earth.

Soaking wet, I stumbled up to the LZ.

"What the hell?" I said.

"We have a team under fire and a missing lieutenant," Tut said. "We are the reactionaries."

"In this weather?" I yelled against the howling wind. "The birds aren't flying, are they?"

Tut smiled. "They said they'd be here in a few minutes."

I was silently cussing myself. Me and my big mouth!

With just weeks to go, here I was standing in the miserable night weather with Tut about to lead me into a nasty place full of lead and little yellow men. At best, we would land in the middle of the night with a bloody fight going on. That's if we didn't crash before we got to the LZ.

Geez, I thought. *I need some professional help.*

Tut could see it my eyes.

"You still want to go, don't you?" That damn cocky smile was wide on his face.

"I said I would, so here I am," I said, trying to sound gung ho.

The team sat buckled against the rain and wind. The only soul I really knew was Tut. I kept thinking that this place had truly snagged my mind and that my love-hate relationship with the bush was going to get me wasted yet. I was so short that it was insane to think about going into the bush. It was too late to become a martyr for freedom or a hero for democracy. But my honor was at stake. There was a team in trouble, and it was my duty to do what I could with Tut and his team to help them. Nevertheless, my throat was tight and my stomach was upside down. Tut just sat there dragging on a smoke, as if the whole deal was just another walk in his park. My apprehension kept building.

And then it happened—the most memorable radio call I can recall in Vietnam. The mission was scrubbed! My 90-proof fear instantly changed to high-octane joy. Tut was laughing. I told him to forget any more ideas about dragging me into the bush. I wouldn't succumb to stupidity in the future. My IQ had finally ratcheted up a notch or two.

"Aw, come on, Fudd," Tut said, still packing that smile. "It would have been fun to have found the lieutenant and rescued the team."

I considered flipping him off, but his brash smile was always contagious. I felt good knowing that I would have gotten on that chopper, and I suppose it could have been a glorious night in the jungle. Tut might have had to pull me off kicking and screaming when we landed, but at least I knew I would have gone. And Tut knew it too.

Word came in the morning that the team and the lieutenant got out of the bush—shot up, but out.

I was transferred to Force Recon to spend my last two weeks. They needed a driver for the commanding officer, and I was the man. I didn't want to go, because it meant I had to get my head shaved. For some daft reason, Force reconners wore boot-camp hair, and mine was almost long enough for me to pass as a civilian. I fought them, but they won.

I ended up getting to know Jimmy Stewart's stepson, First Lieutenant Ronald McLean, who was the company executive officer. He seemed a decent sort. One day I complained to him about my haircut.

"Yeah, I feel the same," he said, "but it is what the CO wants."

After I got home I received news that McLean had been killed about a week after I left.

On my final day, Ernie walked me down to the LZ. I was to chopper down to Da Nang, and then be on my way home. I don't know how I ended up with a bottle of Vodka, but we sat sipping it while we waited for the birds. Ernie was the last one left. Tut had gone to a CAG unit, Mac was gone, and I can't remember where Meatball was.

We made small talk. The elation of knowing I was going home in one piece was almost as consuming as the fear I'd known for so long. I think Ernie was feeling a little lonely. At least I knew that if I were Ernie, I would sure feel alone. It had been a tense time—a time of maiming and death—and I was glad it was coming to an end for me.

I got a little fuzzy as we sipped on the Vodka. The choppers showed up just in time to save me from becoming quite intoxicated. But when I saw the South Vietnamese pilots, I told Ernie to give me another slug of the booze. I couldn't believe the irony: I had never flown with these guys before, and now they were going to provide my very last chopper ride in Vietnam. Today was a very bad day to get wasted.

I handed the bottle to Ernie and shook his hand.

"Do you still want to be buried facedown?" I asked.

Ernie laughed, and I laughed at Ernie.

As usual the bird hammered along above the landscape of Vietnam. It was a beautiful landscape, yet I knew that on the ground grunts were living like animals and that somewhere recon teams were probably getting ready to run like dogs.

I wasn't deep in thought, just totally consumed with getting out of there. So I wasn't ready for the chopper to make a hard banking turn and fall out of the sky. I know that my eyes bulged and my stomach seemed to leave my body. When the door gunner opened up, I tried to accept the fact that I would end up dead. It was the only time I wished I were a Catholic. A Hail Mary is a quick, fast prayer. We Baptists usually make some opening statements to God, and I didn't think there was enough time to do that.

When I saw the wounded deer fall under the hail of gunfire, I was overcome with anger. These blade jockeys had just aged me at least twenty years. Still alive, I now had to go through the ritual of getting my ascending spirit back into my limp body. If you have ever tried to give yourself mouth-to-mouth resuscitation, you will understand my frustration. The adrenaline had poured right out of my ears, and when the relief of understanding hit me, it just about sapped what little blood I had left in my heart. I couldn't believe I was sitting on the jungle floor, inside a chopper, with these clowns blasting at something other than Charlie.

The door gunner ran out, grabbed the little deer, and threw the bloody creature in to the chopper with us. I scooted as far away from it as possible. I was so angry that I wanted to turn the gun on the whole crew.

We lifted off again and flew towards Da Nang Harbor. Once we were over the water, the door gunner kicked the deer out of the chopper and watched gleefully as the carcass tumbled into the water. No wonder this war was dragging on.

The End…
Or will it ever be?

13
A LONG FAREWELL TO ARMS

By the time I got out of Vietnam, the politicians were attempting to find peace with honor, and the war was in a state of de-escalation. The war machine didn't have a place for those of us who had done our tours, so I was discharged early. Just as I'd planned, I'd gotten a real war behind me, and two weeks after my discharge I got married—to a lady I'd met after Sally and I broke up. But I didn't come home a hero of democracy, and I had a hard time finding that summer pasture.

I went to work at a mill in Redmond and stayed there a few months. I still yearned to fly, and I landed a job at Bend Municipal Airport. Starting out as a gas jockey, I was soon offered a job as an apprentice airplane mechanic. I took flying lessons under the G.I. Bill and got my private pilot's license. In 1973 I enrolled in Lane Community College in Eugene to finish my training in aircraft mechanics. I also got my commercial pilot's license, but by then Vietnam vets were coming home, and it was impossible for a rookie like me to compete with former military pilots for jobs.

Because I once had been a cowboy, at the ripe old age of 30, I decided to try my hand in the rough stock event of rodeo. Still lacking some IQ, I started bailing on bulls, and to my surprise, I got so I could go the required eight seconds with some consistency. Then one day a bull launched me during a practice session. My last vertebra was severely damaged, and the doc said that if there were one more micrometer of separation of the vertebrae, I'd be motoring around in a wheelchair. So I decided I'd better give up bull riding.

I was still in reasonable running shape, though, and one of the bullfighters wanted me to help him out. Fighting bulls sounded exciting, and it was. Standing in the dirt with a 1200-pound bull about to explode out of the chute was much like sitting in the dirt waiting for the choppers to come to insert us in the bush. It was the familiar mix of simple fear and a high-octane rush of adrenaline.

Then one day, after fighting maybe a hundred head of snot-throwing bulls, a bull went into a hard spin with a cowboy hanging on the rope. Again my honor was at stake. A grunt was in trouble, and it was my duty to do what I could to free him. My timing was off by one swish of the bull's tail, and the beast caught me with his head right between my running lights. The impact nearly knocked my running shoes off of my feet. Had I been wearing underwear, I'm sure they would have gone airborne as well. The good thing was that, by some mysterious quirk of science, that shock to the cranium did increase my IQ. Now I even have a hard time remembering why in the heck I thought it was important to fight bulls, much less ride them.

To find work, I eventually went back to the timber industry, and I spent twenty years bouncing around as a welder-mechanic in various mills around the Northwest.

Life was okay, but something deep inside of me was nagging at my soul. Early on, letters from Nam came in, and I answered a few of them, but I never wrote Ernie, Mac, Tut, or Meatball. It was strange. If I had it to do over, I would have followed my unit and those I knew were still there. But at that time I wanted to forget. Vietnam had been acid-etched in my memory, but for many years it would almost be forgotten. The mind is a fragile thing. It uses quiet little tricks to stay in one piece. How does the mind hide so well from the soul? I dug a deep hole and pulled the lid over all the senses concerning Vietnam. I talked to no one about it, and no one talked to me. It never really happened.

One night in 1970 Michael Kinnaman arrived home in sorrowful shape. In Vietnam he and his brother, Ron, had both been grunts—one in the Army, the other in the Marines. Three weeks before his rotation, Ron had stepped on a land mine and lost his foot, while Mike had been wounded by manglers during his stint with the Third Marines. Now delayed anger and frustration over Vietnam caused Mike to slam his fist through his parents' living room window. As he stumbled up to bed, he left a trail of blood on the floor. Ron came home a short time later and tracked his brother's blood into the bedroom. He shook Michael awake, and the two got into a fight. Their dad, a WWII Marine veteran, subdued them and calmed them down.

"What the hell was it all for?" Mike asked his dad.

"Money and politics," his father replied.

We really had been mice caught between the hawks and the buzzards.

When the news showed the last moments of our involvement in Vietnam in 1975, I was home alone—and I was glad. Panic-stricken Vietnamese were fleeing the NVA invasion, and choppers were being pushed off the decks of carriers to make more room for them. I went into my bedroom. Honest to God, I tried to cry, but all I could do was produce some mist in my eyes. My pump did make a half-stroke, but the well would not flush the soul. I couldn't believe we had lost the war.

One night in 1985, the manglers exploded in the middle of the night. I jumped up out of bed, ready to run for the holes. When my feet hit the carpet, I came to my senses. I went to the kitchen and drank some water. All was well. It was just a little nightmare. The room was not full of little yellow men.

Outside, a full pure moon cast its light over the pasture of our little ranch.

The manglers came back a few times after that, once or twice I stood over Mac as he lay miserable in that body cast, and once I was captured by the yellow men. A drink of water from the kitchen chased things away.

I struggled with survivor's guilt for a time. I questioned the joy I had felt when I got out of Vietnam in 1969. I questioned everything I had done, everything I had seen, and everything I had said. Had I done my duty to my fullest? Where there times I could have been bolder? Why was I alive and healthy, when so many others were maimed or in the grave? It became a black period of revisiting the past.

This journey was lonely; I couldn't discuss it with anyone. Maybe that's one reason my marriage broke up after fifteen years, but it's hard to say. War had changed me, and I still had a lot to deal with, but it was also a time when many marriages failed.

It took some time to sort things out, but I finally came to the conclusion that each of us are given only so many days here on this earth and that in the days I'd had so far, I had done my duty. The sad fact was that no matter what any of us had done in Vietnam, no matter how many of us were killed or how many medals were handed out, our individual or group performance changed nothing in that dirty little war. When it was over, all we had left was the respect of those who had been there with us. We had become a group of veterans who had only each other to understand, each other to respect, and each other to remember.

I began a convoluted search to find God again. I made the quest difficult because God hadn't gone anywhere. I was the one who had moved. I had blamed God for the war, but I finally realized that man has never figured out how to live in peace. I understood that I had been trying to serve two masters. It is very difficult to live a testament of God's love when you have blood lust in your soul. Soldiers on both sides of the Civil War were undoubtedly God-fearing men. Yet the blood of that war ran deep in this country. God states clearly that we are not to kill one another, yet we continue to do so under the banner of many causes. It is a deep mystery to me, one that could take up reams of paper, and it's still beyond my total understanding. At the very bottom of it, though, is the fact that when you take another man's life, your life will never again be what it once was.

Bury Me With Soldiers

I finally got the courage to call Lieutenant Crary's parents. It was interesting to hear that they had received another call just a week earlier. I found Ernie and gave him a call. He told me that the counseling centers in his area had been jammed. Fifteen years after Nam, our pumps were trying to move water. I asked Ernie if he had heard from Meatball or Mac. He hadn't. We still didn't know if Mac was alive or dead.

Ernie and I reestablished our friendship. I was surprised to hear that he had reenlisted in the Marines after a couple of years as a civilian. When he completed his reenlistment, he went to work as an instrument technician in the Naval Shipyards in Virginia. Ernie wrote to tell me that he had seen an article about Mac in a vet's newsletter. It said Mac was working for the Veterans Administration.

Finding myself on the East Coast in 1992, I visited Ernie and his wife, and Ernie and I took a whirlwind trip to Washington D. C. to visit the Vietnam Memorial. I had heard that visiting it was supposed to be a moving experience. For me it was just a solid piece of rock with many, many names carved in it. It moved me more to see Ernie again. Let it be known, however, that there were no manly hugs, just a strong handshake. It was the 90s, but we weren't 90s-type of guys. I told Ernie that I was very happy he hadn't yet been buried facedown in the dirt and that there was no way I would honor the request he had made in Vietnam.

I'd found Tut about the same time I found Ernie, and I'd given him a call, but I didn't talk to him again until after I had mailed him the original manuscript of this book. After he read it, we started e-mailing each other on a regular basis. We still argue religion from time to time, and Tut still has the same point of view he had in Vietnam. He still calls me Fudd and I still call him Tut. We hope to visit each other one day soon. I can't wait to see that cocky smile again.

One day in 1998, a call from one of the teachers at the local school took me by surprise.

"Wayne, this is Staci. There is a lady who wants to meet you. You were in Vietnam with her husband."

I tried to figure out who had found me in this little town of Condon, Oregon. The only persons I have been in contact with over the years were Ernie and Lieutenant Crary's parents. It had to be Crary's widow. I had often wondered how she had fared after her husband's death.

Staci and I set a time for a meeting in the afternoon. I was all jingled up inside. I couldn't go back to work, so I went home and showered. The clock moved like a slug. Finally it was time. I drove to the grade school and was introduced to the former Mrs. Crary. She gave me a warm, strong hug. Together we went into the seventh-grade classroom and shut the door.

I was at loss for words and choking up a bit. I kicked myself for not bringing a handkerchief. I wanted this woman to know that her husband's men had held him in the highest regard on the battlefield, and I tried to convey to her how defining my short meeting with him had been. I told her that when he was wounded, extreme efforts were made to protect him from further harm. Everything was done to try to save him.

As I wound up the story of my first patrol, I wanted to stand up and give her a full salute. But I didn't think either of us could cope with the emotions that deep gesture of respect would unleash. Both of us held ourselves together, but our runny noses and weeping eyes kept me running back and forth to the sink to fetch some rough old paper towels.

Mrs. Williams told me her story. She told me that Morrell and she had grown up together. Their homes were only a block apart. The day she arrived home from the hospital after giving birth, she had just put her baby girl on the bed when the doorbell rang. Two Marines were standing outside the door. She knew her husband was gone. She went on to tell me that Lieutenant Crary had a signed contract to play baseball with one of the major league clubs. We will never know, but he could have been our generation's hall-of-fame hero.

It was easy to see the pain of her loss, but I could also tell that she had carried on with purpose and dignity. I hoped I had done as well.

A year later, I met Lieutenant Crary's mother, daughter, and one of his grandsons. The meeting went well for all of us. Lieutenant Crary's daughter, Shannon, was perky, and I enjoyed her sense of humor. Mrs. Crary was dignified and, although up in years, possessed of a quick wit and good sense of humor. We talked a little of Morrell's death, but most of the conversation was lighthearted and consisted of swapping information about our respective families.

I did learn that Morrell was an only child and that he could have stayed out of the military. He had wanted to serve his country, as his father and uncle had. His father had served in WWII, and his uncle had been killed in Korea. The will to serve was strong in his family, and Morrell felt this same tug as many others of our generation.

When Shannon made ready to leave for her home, I stood up to shake her hand and the hand of her son. As I clasped the small hand of the three-year-old, a tremor went through me. His facial expression was a mirror of his grandfather's 32 years earlier. I hope someday this youngster and his brother will understand that their grandfather was a man I was honored to have met, a man who will always have a place in the minds of those who served with him.

I offer a heartfelt full salute to this family—a full salute to all families who have endured the highest loss.

In 2002 I spoke with Meatball. He seemed to be doing fine except for some lung damage he sustained as a firefighter in Florida. I asked him if he intended to make any of the reunions that Third Recon Battalion was holding.

"No," he said. "Now, if they'd rent a big field next to a fishing hole and give us buckets to sit on, I might be interested. But I don't like fancy hotels and big cities."

During our conversation, I was afraid I might slip up and offend him by calling him Meatball. Deep down, though, I believe he wears his nickname with the same pride I wear mine. If he doesn't, he should, because there's a rumor flying around Vietnam that Meatball and Fudd are coming back as tourists, and once again the locals are shaking in their sandals.

In Vietnam the term we used when a soldier died was *wasted*. More than 58,000 American soldiers were killed in Vietnam. If they were placed head to toe along one of our freeways, the dead would extend over 70 miles. Bend has a population of about 49,000 people. If you add the outlying areas, the total would probably equal all those killed in Vietnam. That is one entire city wasted.

I've read that Vietnam veterans have committed suicide in numbers that rival those of the soldiers killed in the war. In discussions with families, I've learned of several cases where a Vietnam veteran died after his tour. One simply walked out on the freeway and let the oncoming cars take his life. Another was found drowned in an irrigation canal, and yet another parked his car on the railroad tracks and waited for the train.

I remember one Saturday morning, fifteen years after Vietnam, when I was having coffee with my younger brother Brian. Out of the blue, with absolutely no warning, he said something that I had not heard before.

"I never did thank you for going to Vietnam. I want to thank you now."

The hot coffee stalled in my throat.

I think that the veterans who killed themselves might have wanted to keep living if the nation had esteemed and thanked hem for their offering. In WWI and WWII, American soldiers came home as saviors of freedom, an honor that helped them cover the cost of their sacrifices. There was no hero's welcome for the soldiers who returned from Vietnam.

Even today, disabled Vietnam veterans wake up every morning with the full reminder of their sacrifice. Some are blind, burned, or bound by wheelchairs. As we go about our daily lives, the rest of us forget the daily price they pay. I ask each citizen of this country to pause for a moment and be thankful for these men who answered the call of this country. They are a living testament to honor and courage.

It could be said that we who survived Vietnam are the veterans of a wasted war. I believe that everyone who received medals would have gladly stacked them in the dirt in exchange for a victorious conclusion.

General Westmoreland's plan was to win the war by killing as many of the enemy as possible. That sounded like what most wars are about, but nobody on our side of the fence seemed to understand that the enemy could also count and that they were keeping track of the coffins being loaded in the planes for their trip back to the States. As long as both sides were counting the dead, the goal of the war wasn't to win—it was to see who had the most dead. All Charlie had to do was hammer a little here, bang a little there. Be patient, be smart, keep killing Americans. One day the body count would be so high that they would give up and go home.

Admiral Thomas H. Moore once said, "The only reason to go to war is to overthrow a government you don't like." Apparently our leaders didn't agree with that piece of common sense. They didn't want to overthrow the government of North Vietnam. This, I believe, was what caused the war to drag on with the needless loss of so many lives.

Undeclared wars are open-ended graveyards. If we don't take a conflict to its full, victorious conclusion, we will continually be expending our national treasures of money and lives to police unfinished wars. There must never again be rules of engagement that prevent our military from achieving complete victory. If our leaders start a war, they must let the generals finish it. If they are unable to prosecute the war in this manner, they should let the soldiers stay home.

In 1995 my number-two son called me to say that he had joined the Navy. "I'm going to try to become a Seal," he said.

"Well, you can do it," I said. "Just never say, 'I quit.'"

We talked for a few moments and then hung up. I said I'd call him back soon and discuss this matter with him further.

At the time I had just finished reading about some famous politicians who had wiggled out of the draft. I couldn't believe that such men would be in charge of my son's well-being and in control of his destiny. I felt then, and still do today, that such men have no concept of honor. I knew my son would fight if this country were threatened, but I didn't want him in the hands of the same kind of politicians who got us into Vietnam.

I called Cody and told him my thoughts. I said I would support any decision he made but that I would prefer it if he stayed out of the military. I told him to take some time and think about it. He called back a week later and said he wasn't going to go. I told him I would contact his recruiter and discuss the matter with him. Cody had to take a less than honorable discharge to get out of his commitment.

I never would have thought I would want my children to stay out of the service. I had gone, proud to serve, and I always thought that's the way it would be for my sons. But serving when our national security is threatened is one thing; being used as policeman by the politicians is something entirely different.

This grunt pleads with our national leaders. Our children see and hear the things you do. Search your souls and determine if your actions are for the good of the nation, or for the good of yourselves. Show courage of the highest order as you lead us. Hold on to honor as if it were more valuable than gold. Show us that although you are human, you are capable of honesty and integrity. Prove to us that you possess a strong will to serve, not to be served. Seek peace, but let no man take our freedoms. If we are forced into war, then forge the path for victory. Do not waste our young with mislaid plans. Be willing to send your own sons and daughters into the blood dance. Do not ask for the blood of our flesh if you are not willing to spend the blood of yours.

When we go to war, we offer our grunts to be maimed and killed, and we ask them to maim and kill. We can hope and pray for peace, but we live on a brutal planet. Man will always find a reason to kill. Our nation's leaders must be honorable with the blood they spend. We must hold them accountable for it and know for certain that it will purchase what is right, what is true, what is honorable. Anything less will be another wasteland of deceit.

For me the war in Vietnam has become the men I came to know in it, the kind of men I would like to be buried next to. I can see Tut kicking at the lid of the coffin, trying to snatch the flashlight out of my hands so he can find the Lone Ranger in the dark and pull off his mask. Mac would be so cranky that he'd probably get sent back from death to mellow out a bit. Ernie's strong arms would keep the undertaker from closing the lid until he was certain his radio was nowhere in the vicinity. Meatball would sit up, smile, and ask for a fishing pole to take with him. Me...well, I would just lie there in peace and smile at the company I'd be keeping in the dirt.

A grunt is born in the dirt, makes and loses friends in the dirt, weeps in the dirt, laughs in the dirt, and knows with whom he wants to be buried in the dirt. That is where it all started, and that is where it will end.

The Vietnam veterans of the Third Reconnaissance Battalion are no longer deadly, and most of us have aged to the point of being slower than swift. All of us have been silent too long. We made the offering, and it is time to stand noble, not in conceit, but in humble understanding that our blood was as absolute as any blood before us or any blood since.

I am not a victim of Vietnam. I am a survivor, one who has told this story in the hope that those who read it will understand. Thank you, Ernie, Mac, Meatball, and Tut—it was an honor to serve with you. You didn't choose the war, but you boldly fought the battles.

The grunts—God bless 'em all.

A final note to my family and friends: Please bury me in a set of Marine dress blues. I say this not because I once was a Marine, but because I finally realize that I will always be a Marine. I would like each of my children and my grandchildren to receive an American flag, not as a reminder of me, but as a reminder that America must always be bigger than any individual or group in power. Struggle for this nation; continually ask your leaders to serve you with integrity. Do not let them desecrate the blood of those who have died serving this country. Hold fast your freedoms—there is nothing more precious.

It is a spiritual thing to have served this nation, to have stood with the young and the brave. It will be a spiritual thing to one day stand before Christ and touch his battle wounds. And it would be a spiritual thing to volunteer for a recon mission into the rings of Saturn. Now that would be one outstanding and very cool chopper ride.

Glossary

A-gunner: The machine gunner's assistant. He packs the spare barrel and as much ammo as possible.
Arty: Artillery.
AWOL: Absent without leave. You just don't call in sick in the Marines.
C rations: A full meal deal with canned food such as ham and lima beans, pork steak and ham and eggs. (Add your own sand.) They also included cigarettes, chocolate, instant coffee, and the smallest roll of toilet paper in the world.
CAG: Combined action group. A mix of American and Vietnamese soldiers.
Claymore mine: A portable mine used for defense.
CO: Commanding Officer or your wife.
Company thief: A person who steals from other units to meet the needs of his own unit. This is a critical job that requires stealth, cunning, and speedy lips.
CP: Command Post— the hub of mass confusion and hysteria.
Deuce and a half: A heavy truck, 2 ½ ton rated.
DI: A drill instructor who transforms maggots into soldiers. A split personality is required for the job, and applicants also must have failed at least one course in human relations.
DMZ: Demilitarized Zone (where many battles are fought with invisible armies that are not supposed to be there.)
Frag: Fragmentation grenade. To waste someone with a hand grenade.
Grunt: Anyone who travels by foot. This includes airborne maniacs as well as corpsmen, snipers, and radiomen, because sooner or later they all hit the ground. In the civilian world a grunt is just about the same—the cowboy, the welder, the electrician, etc.
Gunny: Gunnery Sergeant (usually a career marine or someone who loves the Corp more than a private.)
Harbor site: An area that recon Marines used for rest and surveillance posts, marked by a very small defensive perimeter defended by the team and usually a preplotted artillery ring.
Honey bucket: The military sewer system, which consisted of barrels under outhouses to collect human waste. These barrels are removed and the contents burned on a regular basis. This task is often reserved for the new guy or someone causing trouble. (I had to do this once because I got caught standing around with my thumb in the wrong part of my body.)
Hooch: A plywood or tent living area.
Hump: To hike or march.

Jeepie: A jeep left over from WWII in the Philippines and converted into taxis by the locals.
LAW: A Light antitank weapon that looks like a bazooka..
NVA: The North Vietnamese Army.
Remington raider: A military man who works in the office.
Round Eye: A Caucasian female.
RPG: A Russian-made, rocket-propelled grenade.
Section eight: The WWII designation for the rule that provides for discharge on account of a psychological problem.
Spooky: A fixed wing aircraft that carried miniguns that were reported to place a bullet every square inch on a football field.
UDT: WWII underwater demolition teams. Now the Navy Seals
Utilities: The Marine's battle dress with pockets for everything.
Willy-Peter: White phosphorus arty round. Used for a marker round and for burning the enemy. A very nasty round to get hit with.

APPENDIX

C. W. Standiford

FROM A MOTHER'S WELL
By Marilyn Savage

I crossed the busy parking lot, giving only a passing glance in the direction of the young man in the brown sweater and western-cut jeans. As I pushed open the second of two glass doors leading into Payless, it came to me with a start that I had just glimpsed Del. I turned back, pushed by the clutching feeling that always came over me whenever I saw him now. He was gone.

I stood there, as my mind carried me back to that spring of his sophomore year when Del met me at the classroom door.

"My brother's joined the Marines, and Tim's going with him. Now they won't have to take their chances with the draft," he said.

Johnie and Tim were seniors, football teammates, and good friends. As the football coach's wife, I knew most of the players. Del and Ralph, younger brothers to Johnie and Tim, were in my class and had become special friends. Del and I frequently chatted, comparing notes about sports, school, and life in general.

"How do your folks feel about it?" I asked.

"Oh, they're real proud. Dad thinks the only way to get this Vietnam thing over with is to get a lot of good men over there and clean things up."

My own sons were young, and I felt a flash of gratitude that I would have them around for a while yet.

Late May and graduation came, and the two young men, boys no longer, were off to Camp Pendleton for basic training. Del reported that boot camp was tough but so were Johnie and Tim and they were making it just fine. I grew accustomed to inquiring about the progress of the soldiers from their younger brothers. It came as no surprise, then, when Del met in the upstairs hall one afternoon in September.

"Uh, Mrs. Savage," he started, his toe etching the lines on the oiled wood floor in the dimly lit hall. "I just wanted to tell you that Johnie and Tim got their orders for Vietnam. They've already been shipped."

I touched his arm in silent comment. We both knew that Johnie and Tim had volunteered to join the Marines. But we both knew, too, that there really was no choice and that the risk was great.

Weeks passed and months. The small town of Redmond was proud of its two young Marines. They seemed to be a civic contribution to the cause that few understood.

Early in the spring word came, almost inevitably as I look back on it, that Tim had stepped on a land mine. One leg and one arm had been removed and he had lost his eyes. The second leg was not taken off until he was shipped to a hospital in California. His parents made several trips to see him before he died six weeks later.

Johnie's death was perhaps more merciful. He was shot—killed immediately while on routine patrol.

Because they were surviving sons, Del and Ralph were declared exempt from the draft. They completed the school year as outstanding athletes, just as their brothers had done. I continued to talk to Del, only now there was an unspoken bond between us.

The following summer we moved, and my daily visits with Del ended.

Football season came again with the fall. The sports page of the *Oregonian* carried a special feature article for its readers accompanied by two photographs. One showed my husband as the head coach at Redmond High School presenting the Honorary Co-captain Award to Johnie and Tim. The second showed Coach Savage presenting the Honorary Co-captain Award to Del and Ralph,

And I hugged my own two sons closer and tighter.

Bury Me With Soldiers

Reprinted by permission of the Daily Local News, Westchester, Pa., Sunday, July 5, 1998
Remembering a war we all tried to forget
By Kristin Frasch

Holocaust survivors say it's the sound of marching boots that takes them back. For Ernie Cooke, it's the whir of a helicopter—a Huey transporter—overhead. Wherever he is, for that moment he's in the landing zone in Vietnam again, wishing his buddies well on that fateful reconnaissance mission, saying good-bye to friends he'd never see again.

"It was like any other mission; it could have been any one of our teams; it could have been me," said Cooke, a Phoenixville native who served two stints in Nam as a Marine Corps radio operator and now works as an instrument mechanic at a Navy yard in Portsmouth, Va.

Every morning, he and his battalion would walk up to the landing area from their little plywood houses to see who was leaving that day. "It was like a bus stop, buddies going to work. There were eight guys with all of them. One was my best friend, Gary Thomas…."

At 11:30 that morning, someone from the landing pad ran back to camp. The news was grim. The team had been ambushed. "There was one survivor. He had to load the bodies on the helicopter." It wasn't Thomas.

From that day on, Cooke knew what it was to live with death—to accept in a way the "whole life-death process. At 19, he knew what most men at 79 never do. "There is a saying: 'If it doesn't kill, it'll make you strong.' It can also make you stand alone for the rest of your life. When I came home, I felt like I was 100 years old. Even now, if I'm in a roomful of people, I never feel I really belong. I envy people their innocence."

Strength comes in many forms. Sometimes it's just remembering who you are. Hiding under leaves, hovering in foxholes. Buried in the madness that was Vietnam. Cooke would conjure up visions of his town, "give my head a place to go—sitting in the football field, riding around with friends from Phoenixville High, going to Reeves Park." That's where a monument now stands with his name engraved in stone, along with many more from Phoenixville who served or died in Vietnam. In a way, they've all come home there together—guys from one American town whose lives were changed by a war and a country that couldn't fathom it. When Cooke got back, no one talked about Nam, he said. "Even us veterans wanted to forget it ever happened."

But no man forgets the place where his boyhood died along with his buddies. You don't forget what made each of you alive—like Cooke, who played varsity football and ran track—before the death began. That's what hit him at the Vietnam Memorial in D.C.

"Watching mothers and fathers, sisters and brothers find a name and break into tears…. Everybody over there had a town…. Everyone was touched by Vietnam. There is a piece of all of us on that wall."

Only recently have Cooke and others started talking—"most of us seeking answers"—on the Internet, through meetings. There is a brotherhood out there, guys bonded by coming home decades older than their peers, "just trying to be normal, grab a piece of the American pie."

"We're not like those lost vets you see on TV. We're your fathers, brothers, sons. We want to sink into society, have lives again. We stand around at Fourth of July picnics, and no one knows we're any different so long as they don't know all of what we've done, where we've been, what we know."

C. W. Standiford

Bury Me With Soldiers

3rd Recon Battalion Missing In Action

We Pray That One Day They Will All Return Home

The Marines listed were members of the 3rd Reconnaissance Battalion, 3rd Marine Division, United States Marine Corps. All were lost in South Vietnam. Over the years they have each been classified in different categories according to government policy in effect at the time. At the present time all have been declared dead, with a presumptive finding of Killed In Action, Body Not Recovered. Here they are listed as KIA/BNR (Killed In Action/Body Not Recovered), MIA (Missing in Action), or KK (Prisoner of War with Remains Repatriated). Egan, Grissett, and Ibañez were all known to have been captured and taken POW. Egan and Grisset were captured during the same incident. Grissett died in a SVN POW Camp on 02 December 1968. His remains were repatriated and identified in 1989. It is believed that the Viet Cong executed Egan. Ibañez was snatched out of a harbor site by an NVA Patrol. La Porte became MIA after a parachute insertion. The other Marines are all known or believed to have been Killed In Action, and their remains have never been recovered.

21 Jan 66	Capt.	Egan, Jr.	James	T.	1st Force	MIA	4E	81
08 Jul 66	LCpl.	Long a necker	Ronald	L.	Alpha	KIA/BNR	9E	7
18 Aug 66	LCpl.	Rykoskey	Edward	J.	Charlie	KIA/BNR	10E	17
10 May 67	2ndLt.	Ahlmeyer, Jr.	Heinz		Alpha	KIA/BNR	19E	77
10 May 67	HM3	Miller	Malcom	T.	Alpha	KIA/BNR	19E	84
10 May 67	LCpl.	Sharp, Jr.	Samuel	A.	Alpha	KIA/BNR	19E	86
10 May 67	Sgt.	Tycz	James	N.	Alpha	KIA/BNR	19E	88
05 Jun 67	GySgt.	Ibañez	Di	R.	Alpha	MIA	21E	58
11 Jun 67	Pfc.	Chomel	Charles	D.	3rd Force	KIA/BNR	21E	87
11 Jun 67	LCpl.	Christie	Dennis	R.	3rd Force	KIA/BNR	21E	87

C. W. Standiford

Date	Rank	Last	First	MI	Unit	Status	Panel	Line
11 Jun 67	LCpl.	Foley, III	John	J.	3rd Force	KIA/BNR	21E	88
11 Jun 67	LCpl.	Havranek	Michael	W.	3rd Force	KIA/BNR	21E	89
11 Jun 67	LCpl.	Kooi	James	W.	3rd Force	KIA/BNR	21E	90
11 Jun 67	Sgt.	Moshier	Jim	E.	3rd Force	KIA/BNR	21E	91
11 Jun 67	Pfc.	Widener	James	E.	3rd Force	KIA/BNR	21E	93
30 Jun 67	Cpl.	Allen	Merlin	R.	Alpha	KIA/BNR	22E	86
30 Jun 67	HM3	Judd	Michael	B.	Alpha	KIA/BNR	22E	88
30 Jun 67	LCpl.	Killen, III	John	D.	Alpha	KIA/BNR	22E	88
30 Jun 67	Cpl.	Runnels	Glyn	L.	Alpha	KIA/BNR	22E	90
03 Aug 67	HN	McGrath	James	P.	Alpha	KIA/BNR	24E	73
03 Aug 67	LCpl	Nahan, III	John	D.	Alpha	KIA/BNR	24E	73
03 Aug 67	LCpl	Wolpe	Jack		Alpha	KIA/BNR	24E	75
05 Sept 67	HMC	La Porte	Michael	L.	1st Force	MIA	26E	1
05 Sept 67	LCpl	Prather	Martin	W.	Delta	KIA/BNR	26E	3
14 Sept 67	HM3	Wilson	Gary	R.	Alpha	KIA/BNR	26E	73
05 Apr 68	2nd Lt.	Matocha	Donald	J.	Delta	KIA/BNR	48E	15
18 May 68	LCpl.	Padilla	David	E.	Echo	KIA/BNR	66E	22
02 Dec 68	Sgt.	Grissett	Edwin	R.	1st Force	KK	4E	82

Total - 28

UNIT CITATIONS FOR 3RD RECONNAINANCE BATTALION

From the Secretary of the Navy

The Secretary of the Navy takes pleasure in presenting the Navy Unit Commendation to

Third Reconnaissance Battalion (Reinforced)
Third Marine Division (Reinforced)
Fleet Marine Force

For service as set forth in the following citation:

For exceptionally meritorious conduct in the performance of outstanding service in the Republic of Vietnam from 16 September 1967 to 31 July 1968. Assigned the mission of maintaining reconnaissance surveillance for the principal Third Marine Division combat bases at Quang Tri, Phu Bai, Dong Ha and Khe Sanh, the Third Reconnaissance Battalion conducted 1185 reconnaissance missions deep in territory infested by the Viet Cong and North Vietnamese Army. Although the battalion's mission was one of primarily clandestine intelligence gatherings, patrols frequently made contact with the enemy. Though lightly armed, the small reconnaissance units accounted for 606 confirmed Viet Cong and North Vietnamese killed and an undetermined number of wounded; and in addition, located, destroyed, and/or captured enemy harboring and training sites, several large caches of rice, numerous weapons, large quantities of ammunition, and many documents. In addition to the tangible items, the intangible effect of the reconnaissance surveillance in preventing the enemy from massing his forces for a large-scale attack cannot be measured. By vigorous efforts, aggressive spirit, and individual acts of daring heroism, the men of the Third Reconnaissance Battalion, achieved significant and tangible results, and in so doing they exemplified the quality of courage and skill which where in keeping with highest traditions of the Marine Corps and the United States Naval Service.

All personnel attached to and serving with the following units of Third Reconnaissance Battalion (Reinforced) during the period 16 September 1967 to 31 July 1968 or any part thereof are hereby authorized to wear the NAVY UNIT COMMENDATION Ribbon.

Headquarters and Service Company
Company A

C. W. Standiford

Company B
Company C
Company D
Company E
Third Force Reconnaissance Company
Scout Dog Platoon, Force Logistic Command

Secretary of the Navy

3RD RECON BATTALION WAS ALSO AWARDED THE FOLLOWING:

Presidential Unit Citation for the period of 8 March 1965—15 September 1967
Presidential Unit Citation for the period of 20 January 1968—1 April 1968
Meritorious Unit Citation f or the period of 1August 1968—30 September 1968

The President of the United States takes pleasure in presenting the Bronze Star Medal to Corporal **Bruce U. Tuthill**, United States Marine Corps, for service as set forth in the following citation:

For heroic achievement in connection with operations against the enemy in the Republic of Vietnam while serving as a Team Leader with Company E, Third Reconnaissance Battalion, Third Marine Division. On 14 August 1968, Corporal Tuthill was participating in a long-range patrol in enemy controlled territory northwest of the Rockpile. Informed by the point man that he had observed three North Vietnamese Army soldiers moving towards the patrol, Corporal Tuthill quickly positioned his men in an ambush and in an attempt to capture the hostile soldiers, ordered his team members to withhold their fire. With complete disregard for his own safety, he then moved into full view of the approaching enemy and, when they were fifteen feet away, called upon them to defect. When the first man readied his weapon, Corporal Tuthill killed him and as the second soldier attempted to dive for cover, killed him also. Since the third enemy succeeded in reaching temporary shelter, he then requested artillery and air support and skillfully adjusted fire upon possible hostile positions. His heroic actions and resolute determination were an inspiration to all who observed him and provided his unit with valuable enemy equipment for analysis by intelligence personnel. Corporal Tuthill courage, bold initiative and steadfast devotion to duty at great personal risk were in keeping with highest traditions of the Marine Corps and of the United States Naval Service.

For the President,
H.W. Buse, Jr., Lieutenant General, U. S. Marine Corps Command General, Fleet Marine Force, Pacific

    For heroic achievement in connection with operations against the enemy in the Republic of Vietnam while serving as a Patrol Leader with Company E, Third Reconnaissance Battalion, Third Marine Division. On 26 September 1968, Corporal Tuthill was leading a seven-man Reconnaissance patrol in the Ba Long Valley, when the point man observed approximately fifteen North Vietnamese soldiers twenty meters to his front. Reacting instantly, Corporal Tuthill directed his team members to move back and establish a defensive perimeter, and then he and his point man advanced to where they could better observe the enemy. When four North Vietnamese began moving down the trail toward the team's position, unaware of the presence of the Marines, Corporal Tuthill quickly positioned himself and the point man in an ambush. When the hostile soldiers had moved to within five meters of his location, he fearlessly opened fire upon the enemy soldiers, killing the first two while the point man killed the third one. Immediately pressing the advantage of surprise, he rapidly maneuvered his men toward the North Vietnamese, forcing them to retreat by skillful utilization of rifle fire and a grenade launcher. As a result of his exceptional tactical knowledge and bold initiative, his team accounted for a total of four enemy soldiers killed and the seizure of weapons, gear, documents, and what appeared to be a North Vietnamese Army payroll in currency. His heroic and timely actions inspired all who observed him and were instrumental for the Marine's inflicting several losses upon the enemy without sustaining a single friendly casualty. Corporal Tuthill's courage, outstanding leadership and unwavering devotion to duty in the face of great personal danger were in keeping with the highest traditions of the Marine Corps and the United States Naval Service.

Corporal Tuthill is authorized to wear the Combat "V".

The Republic of Vietnam awarded Tut their second highest award. The body of the text reads:

"Exemplary soldier, good battlefield experience, high anti-communist willing.

During operation Lancaster II, began from 1 May to 31 July 1968 in Quang Tri Province, he was overcome under enemy fire, had skill with himself and with his comrades, assaulted to enemy position, causing heavy casualty for the enemy as 744VC/NVA KIA and 176 different types of weapons captured.

This citation was accompanied to award cross of gallantry with bronze star.

Certified a true translation,
Tran Ngoo Thuc

Ernie's citation reads as follows:

For meritorious service while serving as a Radio Operator with Company E, Third Reconnaissance Battalion, Third Marine Division in connection with combat operations against the enemy in the Republic of Vietnam from 6 December 1967 to 10 August 1969. Throughout this period, Private First Class Cooke performed his duties in an exemplary and highly professional manner. Participating in several major combat operations, as well as in more than twenty-four long-range Reconnaissance patrols deep in enemy-controlled territory, he continually supplied his command with valuable intelligence information and repeatedly distinguished himself by his courage and composure under fire. On 10 March 1968, his team was heavily engaged in combat with a large North Vietnamese Army force in the Ba Long Valley of Quang Tri Province. Assuming a forward position to more accurately ascertain the enemy situation, Private First Class Cooke commenced requesting Marine artillery fire upon the hostile unit. Skillfully adjusting the supporting fire, he was instrumental in killing twenty enemy soldiers and forcing the remainder of the hostile unit to retreat. Constantly concerned with the combat readiness of his team, he ably trained his companions in radio operation techniques, thereby greatly enhancing the operational effectiveness of his command. By his initiative, superb professionalism and loyal devotion to duty, Private First Class Cooke earned the respect of all who served with him and upheld the finest traditions of the Marine Corps and of the United States Naval Service.

The combat Distinguishing Device is authorized.

For the Secretary of the Navy,
H.W. Buse, Jr., Lieutenant General, U.S. Marine Corps

Donald Schleman was meritoriously promoted to sergeant, a promotion that required a Marine to show outstanding leadership in combat. Meatball had done just that.

HELP HONOR THOSE WHO HAVE FALLEN

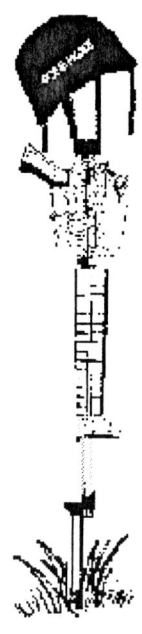

Please tell your friends and family about this book. For every copy purchased a portion of the cover price will be set aside for a fallen warrior's fund. This fund will be for any American citizen direct family member who has lost a father, mother, son or daughter killed in action while serving the United States of America in combat from the Vietnam War forward. The purpose of this fund will be for emergency financial relief and the educational needs of survivors.

America Forever

Wayne Standiford

About the Author

Wayne Standiford lives in the small town of Condon, Oregon, where he works for an electrical contracting company and his wife, Deborah, operates an imprinting business. Wayne and Deborah stay busy taking part in community affairs and keeping track of Shawn, Cody, Cassie, Travis, and Ryan. They are the proud grandparents of Isaac and Wyatt.

Wayne was awarded a Navy Commendation Medal for his "composure under fire" because no one could see his toes curled inside his jungle boots. For the radio incident he was awarded the Vietnamese Cross of Gallantry. This medal should have been an Olympic Gold for the fastest human on the planet on the only day of his life he was able to move really fast. Older and much slower now, Wayne still grunts for a living.

Printed in the United States
38853LVS00004B/24